For all readers,
young and old(er)

ULTIMATE
FOOTBALL HEROES

Matt Oldfield is an accomplished writer and the editor-in-chief of football review site *Of Pitch & Page*. Tom Oldfield is a freelance sports writer and the author of biographies on Cristiano Ronaldo, Arsène Wenger and Rafael Nadal.

Cover illustration by Dan Leydon.
To learn more about Dan visit danleydon.com
To purchase his artwork visit etsy.com/shop/footynews
Or just follow him on Twitter @danleydon

MATT AND TOM OLDFIELD

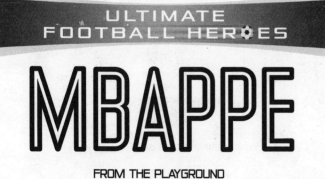

ULTIMATE
FOOTBALL HEROES

MBAPPE

FROM THE PLAYGROUND
TO THE PITCH

DINO

First published by Dino Books in 2018,
an imprint of Bonnier Books UK,
4th Floor, Victoria House, Bloomsbury Square, London, WC1B 4DA
Owned by Bonnier Books,
Sveavägen 56, Stockholm, Sweden

@UFHbooks
@footieheroesbks
www.heroesfootball.com
www.bonnierbooks.co.uk

Design by www.envydesign.co.uk

Paperback ISBN: 978 1 78946 067 4
E-book ISBN: 978 1 78946 111 4

British Library cataloguing-in-publication data:
A catalogue record for this book is available from the British Library.

Printed and bound in Great Britain by Clays Ltd, Elcograf S.p.A.

17

CONTENTS

CHAPTER 1

FROM RUSSIA WITH LOVE

On 14 July 2018, Kylian sent a message to his millions of social media followers, from Russia with love: 'Happy French national day everyone. Let's hope the party continues until tomorrow night!'

'Tomorrow night' – 15 July – the French national team would be playing in the World Cup final at the Luzhniki Stadium in Moscow. It was the most important football match on the planet and Kylian's country was counting on him.

So far, he hadn't let them down at all. In fact, Kylian had been France's speedy superstar, scoring the winning goal against Denmark, and then two more in an amazing man-of-the-match performance against Argentina. That all made him the nation's best 'Number 10' since Zinedine Zidane back in 1998.

That was the year that France last won the World Cup.

That was also the year that Kylian was born.

Thanks to their new young superstar, *'Les Bleus'* were now the favourites to lift the famous golden trophy again. They had already beaten Lionel Messi's Argentina, Luis Suárez's Uruguay in the quarter-finals, and Eden Hazard's Belgium in the semi-finals. Now, the only nation standing in their way was Luka Modrić's Croatia.

'You've done so well to get this far,' the France manager, Didier Deschamps, told them as kick-off approached and the nerves began to jangle. 'Now, you just need to go out there and finish off the job!'

A massive 'Yeah!' echoed around the room. It was one big team effort, from captain Hugo Lloris in goal through to Kylian, Antoine Griezmann and Olivier Giroud in attack. Everyone worked hard and everyone worked together.

By the way, those jangling nerves didn't

belong to Kylian. No way, he was the coolest character around! He never let anything faze him. When he was younger, he hadn't just hoped to play in a World Cup final; he had expected it. It was all part of his killer plan to conquer the football world.

Out on the pitch for the final in Moscow, Kylian sang the words of the French national anthem with a big smile on his face. As a four-year-old, some people had laughed at his ambitious dreams. Well, they definitely weren't laughing now.

'Right, let's do this!' Paul Pogba clapped and cheered as they took up their positions. His partnership with Kylian would be key for France. Whenever Paul got the ball in midfield, he would look to find his pacy teammate with a perfect pass.

Kylian's first action of the final, however, was in defence. He rushed back quickly to block a Croatia cross.

'Well done!' France's centre-back Samuel Umtiti shouted.

Once that was done, it was all about attacking.

Even in a World Cup final, Kylian wasn't afraid to try his tricks and flicks. They didn't always work but it was worth the risk.

It was an end-to-end first half, full of exciting action. First, Antoine curled in a dangerous free kick and Mario Mandžukić headed the ball into his own net. 1–0 to France! Kylian punched the air – what a start!

Ivan Perišić equalised for Croatia but then he handballed it in his own box. Penalty! Antoine stepped up... and scored – 2–1 to France!

The players were happy to hear the half-time whistle blow. They needed a break to breathe and regroup. Although France were winning, they still had work to do if they wanted to become World Champions again.

'We need to calm things down and take control of the game,' Deschamps told his players. 'Stay smart out there!'

Kylian listened carefully to his manager's message. He needed to relax and play to his strengths – his skill but also his speed. This was his chance to go down in World Cup history:

Pelé in 1958,

Diego Maradona in 1986,

Zidane in 1998,

Ronaldo in 2002,

Kylian in 2018?

In the second half, France's superstars shone much more brightly. Kylian collected Paul's long pass and sprinted straight past the Croatia centre-back. Was he about to score in his first World Cup final? No, the keeper came out to make a good save.

'Ohhhh!' the supporters groaned in disappointment.

But a few minutes later, Paul and Kylian linked up again. From wide on the right wing, Kylian dribbled towards goal. Uh oh, the Croatia left-back was in big trouble.

With a stepover and a little hop, Kylian cut inside towards goal but in a flash, he fooled the defender with another quick change of direction.

'Go on!' the France fans urged their exciting young hero.

What next? Kylian still had two defenders in front

of him, so he pulled it back to Antoine instead. He couldn't find a way through either so he passed it on to Paul. Paul's first shot was blocked but his second flew into the bottom corner. 3–1!

Kylian threw his arms up in the air and then ran over to congratulate his friend. Surely, France had one hand on the World Cup trophy now.

Antoine had scored, and so had Paul. That meant it must be Kylian's turn next! He would have to score soon, however, in case Deschamps decided to take him off early…

When he received the pass from Lucas Hernández, Kylian was in the middle of the pitch, at least ten yards outside the penalty area. Was he too far out to shoot? No, there was no such thing as 'too far' for Kylian! He shifted the ball to the right and then BANG! He tucked the ball into the bottom corner before the keeper could even dive. 4–1!

Gooooooooooooooooooooaaaaaaaaaaaaaaaaalllllllllllll llllllllllllllll!!!!!!!!!!!!!!!!!!!!

As his teammates rushed over to him, Kylian had just enough time for his trademark celebration. With a little jump, he planted his feet, folded his arms across his chest, and tried to look as cool as he could. That last part was really hard because he had just scored in a World Cup final!

The next thirty minutes ticked by very slowly but eventually, the game was over. France 4 Croatia 2 – they were the 2018 World Champions!

Allez Les Bleus! Allez Les Bleus! Allez Les Bleus!

Kylian used the last of his energy to race around the pitch, handing out hugs to everyone he saw: his sad opponents, his happy teammates, his manager, EVERYONE! In that amazing moment, he would have hugged every single French person in the world if he could. Instead, he blew kisses at the cameras. From Russia with love!

And Kylian's incredible night wasn't over yet. Wearing his country's flag around his waist, he walked up on stage to collect the tournament's Best Young Player award from Emmanuel Macron.

'Thank you, you're a national hero now!' the French President told him proudly.

'My pleasure, Sir!' Kylian replied.

Would his smile ever fade? Certainly not while he had a World Cup winners' medal around his neck and the beautiful World Cup trophy in his hands. He didn't ever want to let go. Kylian kissed it and raised it high into the Moscow night sky.

'Hurray!' the fans cheered for him.

At the age of nineteen, Kylian was already living out his wildest dreams. The boy from Bondy had become a World Cup winner and football's next great superstar.

CHAPTER 2

A SPORTY FAMILY IN A SPORTY SUBURB

'What if he doesn't like sports?' Wilfried Mbappé whispered to his wife, Fayza Lamari, as they watched their new-born son, Kylian, sleeping peacefully in his cot. He was a man who loved to laugh but at that moment, he had a worried look on his face.

Fayza smiled and spoke softly so as not to wake the baby. 'Does it really matter? Kylian can do whatever he wants to do, and we're going to love him no matter what!'

Her husband nodded but she could still see the frown lines on his forehead.

'Relax, Wilfried, he's our son, so of course he's going to LOVE sports!'

With parents like his, Kylian was always destined

to be a sporting superstar.

Wilfried's favourite sport was football. When he was younger, he had moved to France from Cameroon in order to find a good job. As well as that, Wilfried had also been lucky enough to find the two loves of his life – his wife, Fayza, and his local football club, AS Bondy. His playing days were now over, but he had become a youth team coach instead.

Fayza's favourite sport was handball. She was a star player for AS Bondy in France's top division. Ever since she was a kid, Fayza had been racing up and down the right wing, competing fiercely with her rivals. She couldn't wait to get back out on the court, now that Kylian was born.

'No-one messes with your mum!' Wilfried always told his sons proudly.

Not only were the Mbappés a very sporty family, but they also lived in a very sporty suburb of Paris. Over the years, so many successful athletes, basketball players and footballers had grown up in Bondy. There was top talent on display wherever you turned!

The sports club, AS Bondy, was at the heart of the local community, right in the middle of all the shops and tower blocks. Growing up, Kylian could see the local stadium from the windows of their apartment. It was an inspiring sight.

AS Bondy was a place where people from lots of different French-speaking backgrounds – Algeria, Morocco, Tunisia, Haiti, Togo, Mali, Senegal, Ivory Coast – could come together and enjoy themselves. That was really important because life wasn't easy for the local people. They had to work long hours in order to feed their families and strive towards a brighter future.

For the young people of Bondy, the sports club was particularly special. It was their home away from home, where they could develop their skills, while at the same time staying out of trouble. Coaches like Wilfried taught them three simple rules to live by:

1) Respect each other.

2) Stay humble.

3) Love sport.

At AS Bondy, youngsters could forget about their

problems and just focus on their sporting dreams.

In years to come, the local kids would look up at a big mural showing Kylian's face under the words, 'Bondy: Ville Des Possibles'. No, it wasn't the wealthiest part of Paris, but it was a 'City of Possibilities' where, with hard work and dedication, you could achieve your dreams.

So, what was Kylian's sporting dream? To play handball like his mother, or football like his father? His adopted older brother, Jirés Kembo Ekoko, was already the star of Wilfried's Under-10s football team. Would Kylian follow in his footsteps?

Or perhaps Kylian would choose to play a different sport...

'He can do whatever he wants to do,' Fayza reminded Wilfried, 'and we're going to love him no matter what!'

Growing up, Kylian enjoyed playing tennis and basketball with his friends, but there was really only one sport for him. To his dad's delight, that sport turned out to be football!

CHAPTER 3

THE LITTLE PRINCE OF BONDY

Little Kylian didn't know the meaning of the word 'slow'. He was a football hero in a hurry.

By the age of two, he was already a familiar face in the AS Bondy dressing room. Just as the players were preparing for the match ahead, a little boy would race in with a football tucked under his arm.

'Look who it is – our mascot, the Little Prince of Bondy!' the club president, Atmane Airouche greeted him. 'You're just in time for the team-talk!'

Even if Wilfried wasn't there with him, Kylian was never any trouble. When the manager was talking, he just sat there quietly next to the Bondy players and listened. Before they went out onto the pitch, they all high-fived him. He was their good luck charm.

'Are we going to win today?' the captain asked Kylian.

He nodded eagerly. 'Yeah!'

Kylian would then go out and watch the games with a football at his feet.

By the age of six, Kylian already had his own future all planned out.

'What do you want to be when you're older?' Wilfried asked, recording his son's reply.

'I want to be a footballer,' Kylian said, looking confidently at the video camera. 'I'm going to play for France and I'm going to play in the World Cup too.'

Fayza tried very hard not to laugh at the serious expression on her son's young face. He had such amazing ambition! As the French national anthem played, Kylian sang along with his hand on his heart, just like the players he saw on TV.

'Great, and what club would you like to play for?'

'Bondy!'

Kylian was already training with the juniors. His coach, Antonio Riccardi, was one of Wilfried and

Fayza's closest friends, and so he had been kicking balls around with their sons for years. However, this was the first time that he would see Kylian playing a proper match against kids his own age.

'Wow!' was Antonio's response.

He looked so tiny in his baggy green shirt and shorts, but boy, could Kylian play football!

Even during the warm-up, Antonio could see the difference. He was so much better than everyone else. For a young kid, he really seemed to understand the game. Kylian didn't just kick and chase, like the others; he thought about what he wanted to do with the ball, and then did it. All those weekends at Bondy, spent watching and listening to the adults around him... Kylian had been taking everything in.

'Right, let's practise our dribbling!' Antonio called out.

The coach had set up a line of cones for them to weave through before taking a shot at goal. It looked easy but it wasn't. The first four kids either took it too fast or too slow. They either bumped the ball off cone after cone, or crawled their way down the line like a sleepy tortoise.

'At that speed, you're going to get tackled every time!' Antonio told them as kindly as he could.

At last, it was Kylian's turn and he couldn't wait to show off his skills. He had been working hard on his dribbling at home with his dad and Jirés. It was now time to test himself in front of a bigger audience.

One, two, three, four – as Kylian raced through the cones, the ball stayed stuck to his right foot. His control was so good that he didn't knock a single one of them.

'Excellent!' Antonio called out. 'Now shoot!'

But by then, Kylian was already rushing over to collect his ball from the back of the net. His shot hit the top-left corner of the net before the goalkeeper had even moved.

Kylian was the standout player in the passing practice too. The touch, the movement, the accuracy – it was like he was a professional already! Antonio was blown away by the Little Prince of Bondy. He had coached a lot of impressive kids in Paris, but he had never seen a six-year-old with that much footballing talent. Never!

'Surely he's too good to play with kids his own age?' the coach was thinking, and that was before the match at the end of the session had even started.

'Wow!' Antonio was soon saying again.

To go with his silky ball skills, Kylian also had electrifying pace. It was a winning combination that the poor Bondy defenders just could not cope with. Every time he got the ball, it was goal-time. ZOOM! Kylian was off, sprinting down the right wing, just like his mum on the handball court. Sometimes, he set up goals for his teammates and sometimes, he scored himself.

1, 2, 3, 4, 5, 6–0!

'Okay, let's switch the teams around a bit. Kylian, put on an orange bib!'

6–1, 6–2, 6–3, 6–4, 6–5, 6–6, 6–7, 6–8!

In the end, Antonio had to stop the game early because he didn't want his players to get too down-hearted. Kylian was simply in a league of his own. He was better, faster and more consistent than anyone else.

Once practice was over, Antonio went to find Wilfried.

'I don't think Kylian should be playing for the Under-7s,' he explained.

'Why not?' Wilfried replied, looking surprised. 'Did my son play badly today?'

'NO!' the coach replied, laughing at the idea. 'Quite the opposite; he was absolutely incredible! He's the best I've ever seen at that age. The Under-7s league would be a walk in the park for him; he would just get bored. He needs a challenge!'

By the age of eight, Kylian was playing for the Bondy Under-11s, skilling left-backs all game long. He was on a fast track to the top. His killer plan to conquer the football world was going very well indeed.

CHAPTER 4

FOOTBALL, FOOTBALL, FOOTBALL

'No way, Thierry Henry is the best French player ever!' Kylian argued on the walk home with Antonio. 'Did you not see his goal in the 2006 World Cup semi-final against Brazil? And he hit that on the volley too!'

If the Bondy training session finished before Wilfried and Fayza got home from work, Antonio would often go around to look after Kylian for a few hours. The coach didn't do much babysitting, though. Really, it was just two people talking football, football, football.

'Okay, but who set him up with the free kick in the first place? Zinedine Zidane, without doubt the greatest French footballer of all-time!'

'What about the final, though? France were

drawing 1–1 with Italy when Zidane got himself sent off. He let the whole team down!'

'That's true but who scored France's goal in that final? Zizou!'

'It was a penalty! Henry could have scored that.'

'Maybe, but Zizou won the World Cup for France back in 1998,' Antonio argued back. 'Those two headers in the final against Brazil – unbelievable! Wait, what year were you born?'

Kylian laughed. 'Nineteen ninety-eight!'

The Bondy coach just rolled his eyes. Sometimes, he forgot that he was talking to someone so young. That was easy to do because Kylian wasn't your average nine-year-old. He didn't just play football; he also spent hours watching it, and knew a *lot* about it. He could talk passionately about his heroes for hours.

When they got back to the apartment, they watched football on TV in the living room, while they had some snacks and drinks. After a short sit-down, however, Kylian was back up on his feet again, moving the furniture.

'Hey, what are you doing?' Antonio asked.

'Just getting the football pitch ready!' he replied.

The Bondy coach shook his head. 'No way, your parents will be furious if we break something! Can't you just wait until tomorrow to play outside?'

It was Kylian's turn to shake his head. 'No, it'll be fine. I've got a soft ball and I play here all the time! But you've got to promise that you won't tell Mum and Dad, okay? Promise?'

Antonio found it very hard to say no to Kylian. He let out a loud sigh: 'Fine, I promise, but only for ten minutes!'

Those 'ten minutes' soon turned into thirty entertaining minutes of 'Henry vs Zidane'. It was a miracle that they didn't break anything. One goal was the sofa and the other was the table. There wasn't much space, so it was all about quick feet and quick thinking. Kylian had both of those, plus home advantage. He knew the living room obstacles to watch out for, and the best angles to shoot from.

Time flew until Antonio suddenly looked at his watch and panicked. 'Okay, final whistle!'

'So, I win?' Kylian asked with a smirk. The score

was 10–8 to 'Henry'.

'Yes, this time, but we need to have a rematch soon. Come on quickly, your mum will be home any minute now! You put all the furniture back in the right place, while I clear things up in the kitchen.'

By the time they heard the sound of Fayza's key in the front door, Kylian and Antonio were sitting innocently on the sofa again, as if nothing had happened. They had moved on to their fourth football-based activity of the night – playing FIFA on the PlayStation.

'Hi, Mum!' Kylian called out as the door swung shut.

'Hi darling, how was your day?' she asked, dropping her bag down in the kitchen. When there was no reply, she tried again. 'Kylian, how was your day?'

'Sorry, can't speak right now,' her son replied, tapping the controller furiously. 'Thierry Henry is too busy teaching Zinedine Zidane a lesson!'

CHAPTER 5

CRISTIANO CRAZY!

Thierry Henry was brilliant, but he wasn't Kylian's favourite footballer in the world for long. From 2008 onwards, that was Cristiano Ronaldo. That year, the Portuguese superstar won the Champions League with Manchester United, and Kylian watched every single match on TV.

Like him, Ronaldo was a right winger with lots of speed and skill. He loved to fool defenders with his magical dancing feet. Kylian had never seen anyone do so many stepovers in a proper match. It looked so cool.

'I'm going to do that too!' he decided.

On top of that, Ronaldo was also big and strong. He battled for every ball and his headers were really powerful. That was an area of the game that Kylian needed to work on, and by the time United took on Chelsea in the final, he was Ronaldo's biggest fan.

'What a goal!' Kylian cheered when his hero scored an excellent header in the first half. He jumped up and down on the living room sofa with his T-shirt up over his head.

'Noooooooo!' Kylian groaned two hours later when Ronaldo's penalty was saved in the shoot-out. By then, the boy's T-shirt was back down on his chest, and he buried his face in it.

But no, John Terry missed for Chelsea and then so did Nicolas Anelka. Ronaldo and Manchester United were the winners!

'Yeeeeeesss!' Kylian screamed. His T-shirt was off and he was whirling it above his head like a cowboy's lasso.

Other than AS Bondy, Kylian didn't really have a favourite football team. Paris Saint-Germain were the biggest club in Paris but they were struggling near the bottom of the French league. Instead, he had lots of favourite football players: Henry, Didier Drogba,

Ronaldinho, Lionel Messi, and best of all, Ronaldo.

'Here he comes, "The New Henry"!' Airouche, the Bondy club president, made the mistake of saying one day.

Kylian shook his head firmly. 'No, I don't play like Thierry! I'm a dribbler and a creator, as well as a goalscorer. I'm "The New Ronaldo"!'

'The striker who played for Brazil?'

'No, Cristiano!'

Kylian wanted to know everything about his number one hero. Where did Cristiano grow up? What was he like when he was younger? How did he get so big and strong? Did he have a massive house now, with a cinema room and a swimming pool? What football boots did he wear? What fancy cars did he drive, and how many?

'Once I become a top professional player, I'm going to buy myself TEN beautiful cars!' he told his dad excitedly.

Wilfried rolled his eyes. 'One step at a time, son – you can't get carried away. You'll need to keep improving your skills and you'll need a driving licence too! But football's not about fame and money; it's about success and glory. Has AS Bondy taught you nothing? What's rule number two?'

'Stay humble.'

'That's right!'

Kylian's dad was right; he did still have a long way to go. But Wilfried was wrong about his son's ambition. Kylian's main aim was simple – always to be the best:

The best footballer at AS Bondy…

Then the best footballer in Paris…

Then the best footballer in France…

Then the best footballer in the world, even better than Ronaldo!

The Champions League, the World Cup, the Ballon d'Or – Kylian was going to win them all. The sports cars would just be a nice bonus, a reward for all his record-breaking work.

To keep himself inspired, Kylian decided to decorate his bedroom wall. He pulled out posters from football magazines and cut out images from newspapers too. The action poses changed and so did the kits, but the player in the picture never did.

'It's like a Ronaldo *museum* in here!' Jirés joked. 'You're obsessed, bro!'

Kylian's obsession grew even stronger in 2009 when Ronaldo signed for Real Madrid – for £80 million! It was a new world record transfer fee. After the red of Manchester United and Portugal, Cristiano would now be wearing the famous white shirt worn by the likes of Zizou and the Brazilian Ronaldo.

Kylian had a new favourite football team, and he spent hours watching YouTube videos of his hero's Spanish highlights. Tricks, flicks, free kicks, headers, long-range rockets – there were so many of them! If he kept progressing out on the pitch, Kylian hoped that he too would be worth that kind of money one day. Maybe even more.

CHAPTER 6

CLAIREFONTAINE

By the time Kylian turned nine years old, people in Paris were already talking about 'that amazing boy from Bondy'. At every match he played, there was always a group of scouts watching him.

By the time he turned thirteen, Kylian was ready to take the next big step – joining a top football academy. Playing for AS Bondy was fun, but it was time for a new challenge. After a tough three-day trial, he was one of twenty-two young players from the Paris area selected to attend Clairefontaine.

'You got into Clairefontaine? Wow, that's so cool!' his school friends said enviously.

It was the most famous academy in France and

one of the most famous in the whole world, because that's where French stars Nicolas Anelka, William Gallas and Thierry Henry had all started their careers. For Kylian, joining Clairefontaine felt like a giant leap towards greatness. He was following in Thierry's footsteps!

For the next few years, Kylian would live at the academy from Monday to Friday and then return home to visit his family at the weekends. That sounded good to him, especially when he got to explore the Clairefontaine facilities. It was like a football palace!

They were thirty miles outside Paris in the middle of the French countryside. From his dormitory window, Kylian looked out on beautiful football pitches stretching into the distance for as far as the eye could see. And that was only the start of it. They also had:

An indoor pitch,

A full stadium,

A gym,

And tennis courts too!

'Can I just stay here forever?' he joked with the Clairefontaine coaches.

That was the other amazing thing about the academy. As good as the training had been at AS Bondy with Antonio and his dad, this was ten times better. Kylian was working with France's best youth coaches now, and testing himself against France's best young defenders. Was he good enough to achieve his dream of becoming a professional footballer? That was what he was there to find out.

When Clairefontaine's Director, Jean-Claude Lafargue, watched Kylian in action, he could see the amazing raw talent straight away – the fancy footwork and the incredible pace. However, he knew that talent would need polishing in order to really sparkle at the highest level.

'He's not the best yet,' Lafargue believed, 'but with the right help, he could be!'

The Clairefontaine coaches helped Kylian to improve his weaker foot, so that his dribbling was even more dangerous. If he could take off in either direction, it was so much harder to tackle him.

Stepover to the left, stepover to the right, a little hop, and then GO!

They also helped Kylian to improve his running style so that he was even faster. He still looked a little funny with his long arms swinging, but his teammates weren't laughing when he turned and hit top speed.

'Come on, keep up!' he teased.

Most of all, however, the coaches encouraged Kylian to think about his movement. That was one of the big differences between good players and *great* players. They didn't want Kylian to tire himself out by racing around the pitch. Instead, they wanted him to save his energy for making the *right* runs.

'Look for the gaps!' they shouted.

'What are you going to do when you get the ball?' they asked. 'You've got to be one step ahead of the game!'

'If you can't find space, make space for someone else!' they told him.

Kylian was learning so much, both in the classroom and on the training field, and he was then putting it into practice on the pitch. He scored more and more goals for Clairefontaine and back home at AS Bondy too.

'Watch this!' he told his teammates when he played for them at the weekends. One touch to control the ball and then he was off. *ZOOM – GOAL!*

Kylian was determined to become the best. He was playing more matches than ever but sometimes, that still wasn't enough. He wanted his life to be football, football, football, and even more football!

If he couldn't sleep, Kylian would sneak outside for some extra training. He always kept a ball under his bed just in case. At night, the academy switched their big floodlights off but he used the torch on his mobile phone to guide himself down the stairs and onto the tarmac.

Ahhh! Out in the fresh air, with a ball at his feet, Kylian always felt more relaxed. And with no-one watching him, he could finally practise the latest Ronaldo goal in peace:

'Mbappé has it on the left wing for Real Madrid.

Gerard Piqué and Dani Alves are waiting for him on the edge of the Barcelona penalty area, but he fools them both with one simple stepover. Mbappé dummies to go right, but shifts the ball on to his left foot instead for the shot. BANG! Straight through the goalkeeper's legs....

Goooooooooooooooooooaaaaaaaaaaaaaaaalllllllllll lllllllllllllll!!!!!!!!!!!!!!!!!!!!

He had to whisper all this because he would be in big trouble if the Clairefontaine coaches found him out of bed.

Kylian loved his time at the Clairefontaine academy, but it couldn't last forever. At the age of fifteen, it was time for him to move on to bigger and better things.

Word had spread about Kylian's talent and all the biggest clubs in Europe were queuing up to sign him. He could take his pick, but which one would he choose?

CHAPTER 7

WHICH CLUB TO CHOOSE? PART I

One team hoping to sign Kylian was Rennes. They weren't one of the biggest or richest clubs in France but they had one major advantage – his older brother was already playing for their first team.

'You and me in the same amazing attack,' Jirés tried to persuade him. 'Think how many goals we could score together!'

It was certainly a tempting idea. Kylian knew the club really well. When he was seven, he used to practise his skills on the pitch next door, while Jirés played for the youth team. Everyone at Rennes remembered the little boy from Bondy who always had a football at his feet.

Six years on and people were calling that boy the 'next Henry'. Would he sign for Rennes? Perhaps not, but it was definitely worth a try.

'Would your son like to play for us in a tournament?' one of the coaches asked Wilfried.

'Sure!' said Kylian. He never said no to football.

Wearing the red Rennes shirt, Kylian was head and shoulders above the rest. Once he got the ball, he was simply unstoppable.

'What a player!' the club's coach said enthusiastically. 'We'd love to sign your son for our youth team.'

Wilfried, however, was in no rush to decide. He wanted to make sure that Kylian chose the right club where he would be happy, as well as successful.

'Thank you, we have a lot of offers to consider,' he replied politely.

One of those other offers came from the 2010 Premier League Champions, Chelsea. They sent their scouts all over Europe, looking for the top young talent around. Kylian was soon on their radar and they invited him to come to London for a trial.

'Sure!' he said. He never said no to football.

Kylian loved his time at Chelsea. It was his first experience of being at a big club, and he walked around in a daze.

Wow, the training ground was amazing!

Wow, the Stamford Bridge stadium was really cool!

Wow, there was Didier Drogba, one of his childhood heroes!

Kylian got to meet Drogba, and he got to play some football too. He starred for the Chelsea youth team as they beat Charlton Athletic 8–0.

'You and me in the same amazing attack,' their striker Tammy Abraham tried to persuade him. 'Think how many goals we could score together!'

It was certainly a tempting idea.

'What a player!' the Chelsea coaches said enthusiastically. 'We'd love to sign Kylian for our youth team.'

But still, Wilfried was in no rush. 'Thank you, my son has a lot of offers to consider,' he replied politely.

Kylian left London with happy memories and a

blue Chelsea shirt with his name and Number 10 on the back. That was soon on display on his bedroom wall, next to all the Cristiano posters.

So, what other offers did Kylian receive? Well, every single club in France wanted to sign him, plus Bayern Munich, Manchester City, Manchester United, Liverpool, and even Real Madrid!

The Spanish giants were one of the biggest and richest clubs in the whole world and they had two other major advantages:

1) French legend Zinedine Zidane was their manager

and

2) Cristiano Ronaldo was their star player.

Zidane invited Kylian to come and spend his fourteenth birthday at Real Madrid.

'Sure!' he said. He never said no to football.

It was the best birthday present ever! When Kylian arrived at Real, Ronaldo didn't say to him, 'You and me in the same amazing attack. Think how many goals we could score together!' However, the boy did get his photo taken with his hero.

It was a moment that Kylian would never, ever forget. Wearing a white Real Madrid tracksuit, he stood there smiling next to Cristiano Ronaldo. The superstar even put his arm around his shoulders. No, it wasn't a dream – he had the picture to prove it!

Kylian spent a week at the Real Madrid academy, training with some of the best young players in the world. It was another amazing experience, and it confirmed what he and his family had known all along – that he could compete at the highest level. One day, he was going to be the best.

'What a player!' Zidane said enthusiastically. 'We'd love to sign your son for our youth team.'

Kylian had an offer from Real Madrid, but still, Wilfried was in no rush. 'Thank you, my son has a lot of offers to consider,' he replied politely.

It was going to be the biggest decision of Kylian's young life. Was he really ready to leave France behind? During his time at the Clairefontaine academy, he could go home to Bondy every weekend. If he moved to Madrid, however, Kylian would be much further away from his friends and family. That was a lot for a fourteen-year-old to deal with. But at the same time, could he really say no to Real, Ronaldo's team?

'Remember, it's not "now or never",' Fayza reassured her son. 'There'll be other opportunities. If you don't want to go there yet, no problem. Maybe you'll go there when you're a bit older!'

CHAPTER 8

MOVING TO MONACO

Kylian's mind was made up. For now, he was going to say no to Real Madrid and stay close to his friends and family in France. He was going to sign for a top team with an amazing academy, where he would have the best chance of progressing quickly into the first team.

For all of those reasons and more, Kylian chose Monaco.

The Monaco youth system was the best in the whole of France. The Red and Whites had more scouts in Paris than any other Ligue 1 club, including the local team, PSG! And the Mbappé family had known those scouts for years, ever since Kylian's early days at AS Bondy. They were friendly people, who really seemed to care about his footballing future.

'Your son could be Monaco's next superstar!' they kept telling Wilfried and Fayza.

Kylian's parents had no doubts about that, but was it the right club for their son? Yes! When Kylian visited the Monaco academy centre, 'La Turbie', he was very impressed. The facilities were as big and modern as Chelsea or Real Madrid.

It was also an academy with lots of history. In the past, La Turbie had produced four of France's 1998 World Cup winners – right-back Lilian Thuram, central midfielder Emmanuel Petit, plus strikers David Trezeguet and, you guessed it, Thierry Henry!

'We want to make Kylian the next famous name on that list,' the Monaco academy director told the Mbappé family during their tour. 'This is the best place for him to develop that incredible talent.'

Sold! Kylian loved the sound of that plan. It was the offer that he had been hoping for.

'Welcome to France's greatest football club!' the academy director said, shaking his hand.

At the time Kylian joined their academy, however,

Monaco hadn't won the French league title for thirteen years. In fact, in 2011, they had even been relegated down to Ligue 2. Thankfully, a Russian billionaire called Dmitry Rybolovlev had bought the club and taken them back to the top flight.

'I'm going to lead Monaco to glory again!' Kylian declared confidently.

The club had just spent nearly £100 million on Colombian stars Radamel Falcao and James Rodríguez, but that didn't mean that they didn't care about their young stars. Layvin Kurzawa, Yannick Carrasco, Valère Germain and Anthony Martial had all made the step up from Monaco B to the Monaco first team.

'That'll be me next!' Kylian announced as soon as he arrived.

He couldn't wait to impress his new coaches and teammates. He had a lot to live up to, especially that nickname – 'The New Henry'. Kylian didn't mind the pressure, though. He was sure that he could handle it, even at a higher level.

He wasn't going to let anything stop him from achieving his goals. He always wanted to be the best.

Every time he got the ball in training, he attacked at top speed. ZOOM! He wasn't a show-off, but what was the point in having such silky skills if he wasn't going to use them?

'Excellent, Kylian!'

Leaving his marker trailing behind, he lifted his head up and looked for the pass, just like they had taught him to do at Clairefontaine. If someone was in space, he set them up to score.

'Cheers, Kylian!'

If not, he took the shot himself, and he hardly ever missed.

'Great goal, Kylian!'

Was the Monaco manager, Claudio Ranieri, watching? Kylian hoped so. His masterplan was simple but highly ambitious. He didn't want to sit around and wait patiently. By the end of his three years in the academy, he aimed to be playing for the first team. That seemed realistic to him; it was why he had chosen Monaco in the first place.

If Thierry could do it at seventeen years old, then so could Kylian.

CHAPTER 9

FIRST-TEAM FOOTBALL

After a strong start, however, Kylian's Monaco master-plan was in danger of falling apart. The last of his three academy years had started, and his first-team dream still seemed miles away. Did Monaco's new manager, Leonardo Jardim, even know that he existed? Every day, Kylian grew more and more impatient.

'I don't get it!' he moaned to Jirés. 'What am I doing wrong?'

For years at AS Bondy and Clairefontaine, Kylian had been the coach's favourite and the star player, but not anymore. The Monaco Under-18s manager didn't seem to rate him at all. He was always criticising Kylian for something.

'Track back and help your team!'

'Stop giving the ball away. Pass!'

'Think about what you're doing!'

Kylian was doing his best to improve his game, but his coach's comments were affecting his confidence. At this rate, Monaco might not even offer him a professional contract anyway. He knew that Jirés would understand his frustrations.

'All you can do is try to ignore it and keep working hard,' his older brother told him. 'Everything will work out in the end!'

Those turned out to be very wise words. Kylian's time was coming, and sooner than even he could have predicted.

By 2015, Monaco had stopped spending lots of money on foreign players. That plan wasn't working because the club couldn't compete with PSG in the transfer market. So instead, the club's vice-president Vadim Vasilyev and technical director Luis Campos decided to focus on developing their young French talent. Local players were a lot cheaper and, potentially, a lot better.

One day, while Vasilyev was working on this new idea, he had a visit from a Monaco academy coach, who looked troubled.

'What's wrong?' the vice-president asked.

'We have a talented kid in the youth team, and I think he's going to be a star,' the coach explained.

'Great, what's his name?'

'Kylian Mbappé.'

'Okay, so what's the problem?' Vasilyev asked, looking confused. 'Let's give him a contract!'

Unfortunately, it wasn't that easy because Kylian wasn't very happy at Monaco. He didn't feel wanted by the club and he could no longer see a clear path to the first team.

Plus, he was in high demand once again. He had lots of offers to consider before he signed his first professional contract. PSG were desperate to steal him away from Monaco, and so were Arsenal and RB Leipzig.

Vasilyev went to La Turbie to find out what all the fuss was about. It didn't take him long. Within five minutes, the Monaco vice-president could see that Kylian had phenomenal talent. It wasn't just the speed and the skill; it was also the confidence, the competitive spirit, the fire in the young man's eyes. He seemed to have everything that a young player needed to succeed, and more.

'Wow, why am I only just hearing about this wonderkid?' he thought to himself.

That didn't matter now; what mattered was keeping Kylian happy at Monaco. They couldn't let him leave, especially for free! Vasilyev and Campos went to speak to Wilfried and Fayza about what they could do to help.

'Kylian wants to play first-team football,' his dad said. 'It's as simple as that. I know he's only sixteen, but my son is very ambitious. And very talented!'

Vasilyev and Campos nodded. 'Absolutely, he's one of the most talented young players we've ever seen. Leave it with us; we'll arrange for him to start training with the first team as soon as possible.'

Kylian's first chance came in November 2015. A lot of Monaco's stars were away on international duty, so Jardim needed to call up extra players to take part in the first-team training sessions.

'Get Mbappé,' Vasilyev told him. 'Trust me, you'll be impressed!'

Kylian was so excited when he heard the good news. At last! He didn't feel nervous at all as he walked into the first-team dressing room, and then out onto the first-team training pitch. He believed in himself. This was where he belonged. He couldn't wait to show Jardim what he'd been missing.

ZOOM! Kylian flew past Monaco's experienced defenders in a flash. Now, he had to make sure he finished his run with either a goal or an assist. He had to be more consistent; that was what the Under-18s coach was always telling him. Kylian lifted his head up – did he have a teammate to pass to? No, they couldn't keep up. He would have to go it alone.

The last man backed away, wondering which way Kylian would go…

Stepover to the left, stepover to the right, a little hop, and then GO!

Kylian sprinted into space and fired the ball past the keeper.

Goooooooooooooooooooaaaaaaaaaaaaaaaaalllllllllll llllllllllllllll!!!!!!!!!!!!!!!!!!!!!

Jardim was blown away by Kylian's performance. 'Wow, why am I only just hearing about this wonderkid?' he asked Vasilyev.

The vice-president laughed, 'I asked exactly the same question when I first saw him play!'

'Well, he's not going back to the youth team,' Jardim decided straight away. 'He's a Monaco first-team player now.'

CHAPTER 10

"THE NEW HENRY"

Some young players spend a long time, training with the first team, before they make their senior debut, but not Kylian. He was a hero in a hurry, and who was going to stop him? In December 2015, less than a month after his first training session, he was taking his seat on the Monaco subs' bench!

They were playing at home against AS Caen at the Stade Louis II. The stadium could hold up to 18,000 supporters but it was only ever full for the big games against rivals like PSG. There were only 5,000 in the crowd to watch Kylian's debut against Caen. Well, that was if Jardim brought him on...

'Man, you could make history tonight!' his

teammate, Tiémoué Bakayoko, told him as they watched the first half.

Kylian just smiled and nodded. It was what he had always wanted to do – break records. If he did get onto the pitch, he would become Monaco's youngest-ever first-team player. He was still eighteen days away from his seventeenth birthday. And whose record would he be breaking? Yes, Thierry Henry! That would make it extra special.

Monaco had been struggling to score goals all season. They took the lead against Caen but with five minutes to go, Ronny Rodelin grabbed an equaliser. 1–1!

A draw wouldn't do, though; Monaco needed to win. Jardim turned to his bench. He had already brought on his Portuguese winger, Hélder Costa. Who else did he have?

Paul Nardi – a goalkeeper,

Andrea Raggi – a defender,

Gabriel Boschilia – a midfielder,

Tiémoué – another midfielder,

And Kylian!

Playing a sixteen-year-old was always a risk, but
Jardim reasoned that Kylian's speed and skill could
be deadly against the tired Caen defence. He was the
best option that Monaco had.

'Kylian, get ready,' one of the coaches shouted,
passing on the manager's message. 'You're coming on!'

On the touchline, Kylian tucked his red-and-white
33 shirt into his shorts and waited for the fourth
official to put the numbers up. Monaco were going
all-out attack. Kylian would play on the left wing in
place of the left-back, Fábio Coentrão.

'Good luck, kid,' Fábio said as they high-fived. 'Go
cause some trouble!'

'I'll try!'

Within seconds, Kylian was on the ball. He
controlled Bernardo Silva's pass and then thought
about taking on the Caen right-back. Surely he
could speed straight past him? No, not quite yet. He
decided to play it safely back to Bernardo instead.

'Next time!' Kylian thought to himself.

When Bernardo passed to him again, Kylian
faked to cut inside but then – ZOOM! – he dribbled

down the wing instead with his dancing feet flying. Eventually, a defender tackled him, but the Monaco fans were impressed already.

'That kid looks brilliant!'

Kylian kept moving and calling for the ball. He wanted it every time. He had the composure to pick out good passes, and the strength to go shoulder to shoulder with his opponents. He was totally fearless. In the end, Kylian couldn't grab the winning goal but that night against Caen, his potential was recognised, and a superstar was born.

'Nothing fazes you, does it?' Tiémoué laughed as he congratulated Kylian at the final whistle. 'You were awesome out there!'

Monaco's wonderkid wasn't getting carried away, though.

'Yes, but we didn't win,' he replied, 'and I didn't score.'

Kylian had been dreaming about his first senior goal since he was four years old. How would it feel? How would he celebrate? And what kind of a goal would it be?

It turned out to be a left-foot shot from near the penalty spot. In the last minute of a home match against ESTAC Troyes, Hélder crossed from the left. There were two players waiting for it – Tiémoué and Kylian. He had sprinted all the way from the halfway line to get there first in a blur of orange boots. He was so determined to score.

Goooooooooooooooooooooaaaaaaaaaaaaaaaaalllllllllll lllllllllllllll!!!!!!!!!!!!!!!!!!

3–1! As his shot hit the back of the net, Kylian turned and threw his arms up in the air. Not only was it his first goal but he had made Monaco history again. Seventeen years and sixty-two days – he was now the club's youngest-ever goalscorer. And whose record had he be broken? You guessed it, Thierry Henry! That made it extra special.

'Fair enough, you finished that well,' Tiémoué laughed as they celebrated, 'but next time, it's my turn!'

Although Kylian was clearly enjoying himself out on the pitch for Monaco, he still hadn't signed his first professional contract. That was a major worry for Vasilyev. Had the club done enough to persuade Kylian to stay? Or would PSG steal him away by offering more money and fame?

No, on 6 March 2016, Kylian sat down to sign a three-year deal with Monaco. He was where he wanted to be – playing regular first-team football. He wasn't yet playing every minute, but he *was* playing lots of minutes.

'I'm very happy and very proud to sign my first professional contract,' Kylian told the club's website. 'This is the club that has helped me grow. I feel good here.'

'Right, let's start winning some trophies!' Kylian told his teammates.

Monaco finished the 2015–16 season in third place in Ligue 1, a massive thirty-one points behind the champions, PSG. Still, the good news was that they qualified for the Champions League. Kylian was super-excited about that. Even in the thirty-five minutes of Europa League football he had played against Tottenham, he had managed to set up a goal for Stephan El Shaarawy.

Kylian couldn't wait for the challenge of the Champions League. It was the ultimate test for any football superstar. Who knew, maybe he would even get to play against Cristiano Ronaldo's Real Madrid!

Kylian's youth team days at Monaco weren't quite over yet, though. The Under-19s were through to the final of the Coupe Gambardella against Lens, and they needed their seventeen-year-old wonderkid.

'Sure!' said Kylian. He never said no to football.

Back in Paris at the Stade de France, he was Monaco's matchwinner. He set up the first goal for his strike partner Irvin Cardona with a wicked, no-look pass. 1–0!

The second half, however, was The Kylian Mbappé Show. He used his pace and power to get past the Lens defence and then nutmegged their keeper. 2–0!

Gooooooooooooooooooooaaaaaaaaaaaaaaaallllllllllll llllllllllllllll!!!!!!!!!!!!!!!!!!!

But Kylian had saved his best skills until last. On the edge of the penalty area, he had four defenders surrounding him. Surely, he couldn't escape with the ball! But with a stepover and a burst of speed, he did escape, and he scored too. 3–0!

'Man, you're so good it's not fair!' Irvin joked.

As Monaco lifted the cup, Kylian cheered and bounced up and down with his teammates, but he always kept one hand on the trophy. He didn't want to let it go, even though it would be the first of many.

CHAPTER 11

EUROPEAN CHAMPION

By July 2016, Kylian had become a star for club
and country. Because of his parents, he could have
chosen to play for Cameroon or Algeria, but instead,
he picked France. After all, that was where he was
born and where he had lived his whole life. It was
the French national anthem that a young Kylian had
sung loud and proud with his hand on his heart.
Plus, he wanted to be 'The New Henry'.

'If they want me, I want to play for *Les Bleus*,'
Kylian decided.

So, did they want him? Kylian played two
matches for the Under-17s but after that, his France
career stalled. The Under-18s coach, Jean-Claude

Giuntini, refused to select him. Just like his old
Monaco youth coach, Giuntini thought Kylian was
too inconsistent, too selfish, and not a team player.

Giuntini passed that on to the Under-19s coach,
Ludovic Batelli, but luckily, he didn't listen. Yes,
Kylian was still only seventeen years old, but he
was already lighting up Ligue 1 with Monaco. Plus,
Batelli really needed a new superstar because he had
just lost his best player, Ousmane Dembélé, to the
Under-21s.

'Come on, kid, let's see what you can do,' the
coach told Kylian.

France were in the middle of qualification for
the Under-19 European Championships. Only eight
teams would make it to the big tournament in
Germany. To get there, France needed to win their
last three matches against Montenegro, Denmark
and Serbia. Batelli's team had a strong core – Issa
Diop in defence, Lucas Tousart and Ludovic Blas in
midfield, Jean-Kévin Augustin in attack – but with
Ousmane gone, they lacked flair. That's where Kylian
came in...

'Welcome to the squad,' said Lucas, the captain. 'I've heard amazing things about you!'

Not only was Kylian the newest member of the squad, but he was also the youngest. Would he struggle to make friends? No, because he'd been playing with older age groups all his life.

'Are you sure you're only seventeen?' Jean-Kévin joked. 'You act more like you're *seventy-seven*, if you ask me!'

Kylian didn't play football like a seventy-seven-year-old, though. In the match against Montenegro, he was France's danger man. Whether he popped up on the left wing or the right, he was always a threat. He could and should have got a hat-trick of goals and a hat-trick of assists. But instead, it was Ludovic who scored the only goal of the game.

'Come on, where's the end product?' Kylian asked himself angrily. 'You've got to do better than that!'

He did, two days later against Denmark, scoring the first goal in a 4–0 thrashing. Now, France just needed one last win.

Against Serbia, Jean-Kévin dribbled forward and passed to Kylian out on the right wing. 'Finish this!' his brain was telling him. He took one touch to control the ball, then looked up and BANG!

Goooooooooooooooooooaaaaaaaaaaaaaaaaallllllllll llllllllllllllllll!!!!!!!!!!!!!!!!!!!!

Kylian and Jean-Kévin high-fived. 'We're off to Germany!' they cheered together.

On the touchline, Batelli punched the air. His decision to pick Kylian was really paying off. Could France now go on and win the Under-19 Euros? Why not? The last time that *Les Bleus* had won it was 2010, when they had Antoine Griezmann and Alexandre Lacazette in attack. Now, they had Kylian and Jean-Kévin.

France were placed in Group B with England, Croatia and the Netherlands. Kylian never worried too much about his opponents. At his best, he knew that he was good enough to beat anyone. Unfortunately, he wasn't at his best in the first game against England. Batelli took him off after sixty minutes as France lost 2–1.

'Don't worry, we all have bad days,' his coach told him. 'In three days, we go again!'

Jean-Kévin scored France's first goal against Croatia, and Kylian scored their second. He controlled Issa's long ball beautifully, dribbled around the keeper and tapped it home. He made it look so easy.

Goooooooooooooooooooooaaaaaaaaaaaaaaaaallllllllllll llllllllllllllll!!!!!!!!!!!!!!!!!!!!

'That's more like it!' Kylian shouted passionately as he sank to his knees on the grass.

There was no stopping France now, and especially their star strikeforce. They had a friendly rivalry going. Who could score more? Against the Netherlands, Kylian got two, but Jean-Kévin got three!

'I win this time,' the hat-trick hero said as he walked off with the matchball.

In the semi-finals against Portugal, it was Kylian's turn to shine. France were 1–0 down after just two minutes, but they fought back quickly. Dribbling way out on the left wing, Kylian looked like he was going nowhere. But suddenly, ZOOM! – he muscled his way past the Portugal right-back and played a great cross to Ludovic. 1–1!

'Come on!' Kylian cried out as the whole team hugged each other.

In the second half, Clément Michelin crossed from the right, and Kylian poked the ball in.

Goooooooooooooooooooooaaaaaaaaaaaaaaaaaalllllllllll llllllllllllllll!!!!!!!!!!!!!!!!!!!!

2–1! He celebrated like his hero, with a jump and a spin.

'Nice one, Cristiano!' Ludovic teased.

Kylian's second goal was more like Ronaldo, though. He jumped up high to head the ball past the Portugal keeper. 3–1!

He was France's hero, leading them through to the European Championship final against Italy.

'Okay, you win this time,' Jean-Kévin admitted.

With one game to go, France's two top young attackers were tied on five goals each. Who would claim the Golden Boot?

Against Italy, Jean-Kévin scored his sixth goal in

the sixth minute of the match. 1–0 to France!

What about Kylian? He dribbled into the Italian penalty area, but his shot went wide. 'No!' he shouted, slapping his leg in frustration.

In the end, it was Jean-Kévin who got the Golden Boot and Best Player awards. Never mind that, though, because after a 4–0 win, France were the European Champions! And at the age of seventeen, Kylian had played a massive part in their success. He had another winners' medal to add to his collection.

'Well done!' Kylian's proud parents shouted when they met up with him afterwards.

'Great work!' said the AS Bondy president, Atmane Airouche, who congratulated him. He had come all the way to Germany to cheer his old player on. 'I hope you're having a big party tonight!'

Kylian shrugged. 'Some of the others are going out, but I'm tired. I might just go to bed.'

For Kylian, it was just another goal achieved. The next day, he would move straight on to his next target – winning more trophies at Monaco.

CHAPTER 12

HAT-TRICK HERO

In the space of six short months, Kylian had
played his first senior game, scored his first senior
goal, signed his first senior contract, and won the
Under-19 European Championships with France. All
of that, and he was still only seventeen!

So it was no wonder that Kylian was feeling pretty
confident as the 2016–17 Ligue 1 season kicked off.
He felt ready to fight for more game-time at Monaco.
He would show Jardim that he deserved to play more
than just the last twenty minutes of matches. He
wanted to play every minute of every match! To do
that, though, he needed to start the new season with
a BANG!

Kylian couldn't wait for the first game against

Guingamp. He was starting up front alongside
Guido Carrillo, with Tiémoué and Thomas Lemar in
midfield. Awesome! However, it soon turned into a
nightmare.

First, Monaco went 2–0 down, and then as Kylian
tried to turn things around for his team, he suffered a
head injury and had to come off.

'What? No, I'm fine to play on!' he argued, but
the team doctors stood firm. He couldn't continue in
case there was a serious concussion.

For the next two months, Kylian had to wait and
watch from the sidelines. Monaco were playing well
without him, and they even beat PSG. When would
Jardim put him back into the team? Kylian was still
as impatient as ever.

Kylian finally returned to the starting line-up
against Montpellier. Great, so what could he do to
keep his place this time? As he dribbled into the
penalty area, he had two defenders in front of him
and no teammate to pass to. He faked to cross with
his right foot but then switched it to his left. Just as
he was about to shoot, one of the defenders fouled

him. *Penalty!*

'Well done, mate!' Radamel Falcao said, helping him back to his feet.

Kylian scored Monaco's second goal himself with a clever flick header, and then set up the fourth goal for Valère Germain.

Surely Jardim couldn't drop him after that? But for the next two months, Kylian was in and out of the Monaco team. He would play one great game, and then one average game. That wasn't good enough. He knew that he needed to become more consistent with his goals and assists – and December 2016's League Cup match against Rennes was a good place to start.

Kylian sprinted onto Boschilia's through-ball and curled a shot past the keeper.

Goooooooooooooooooooooaaaaaaaaaaaaaaaallllllllllll llllllllllllllll!!!!!!!!!!!!!!!!!!!!

1–0! 'Come on!' he roared, pumping his fist at the crowd.

Just ten minutes later, Kylian tapped home Nabil Dirar's cross. 2–0!

'Nice one!' he cheered, jumping into Nabil's arms.

Kylian had seventy more minutes to complete his first professional hat-trick. Surely he could do it. The time ticked by quickly, but he didn't give up hope. All he needed was one chance. Finally, in the second half, João Moutinho played the perfect pass and Kylian couldn't miss. 4–0 – he was a hat-trick hero!

'Thanks!' Kylian called out, giving João a high-five and a hug. What a way to celebrate his eighteenth birthday, which was just days away!

Now, Kylian needed to take that red-hot scoring form back into Ligue 1. There was no time to waste. Against Metz, he lined up alongside João, Radamel, Boschilia, Bernardo *and* Fabinho – what an awesome attacking team! Yes, Kylian had a very good feeling about this game...

João chipped a great pass over the top to Radamel, who headed it down to Kylian. With his left foot, he calmly placed his shot in the bottom corner. 1–0!

Goooooooooooooooooooooaaaaaaaaaaaaaaaalllllllllll lllllllllllllll!!!!!!!!!!!!!!!!!!!!

'Thanks, partner!' Kylian cheered happily, pointing

back at Radamel.

They were Monaco's new star strikeforce, just like Kylian and Jean-Kévin had been for the France Under-19s. Kylian's speed and skill, combined with Radamel's strength and experience – what could defenders do? Uh oh, Metz were in big trouble.

Radamel converted a cross from the right. 2–0!

Kylian raced onto Fabinho's long ball, cut onto his right foot and scored. 3–0!

'Come on!' he cried out, punching the air.

It was time to score another hat trick. Boschilia threaded a great pass through to Kylian. As the goalkeeper rushed out at his feet, he managed to poke it past him. 4–0 – hat-trick hero!

Kylian stood there with his left arm in the air and a huge grin on his face. What a feeling! The Monaco fans waved their red-and-white flags and chanted his name:

Mbappé! Mbappé! Mbappé!

There was even time for Radamel to grab a second goal. 5–0!

'If we keep this up, the title's ours for sure!' Kylian

cried out joyfully.

They were playing so well together. With thirteen games to go, Monaco were top of the Ligue 1 table, three points ahead of their rivals, PSG. The fans were full of hope, after seventeen years of disappointment. Kylian and his teammates couldn't let them down.

'Let's take it one game at a time,' Jardim told his players, 'and take our chances!'

Kylian did exactly what his manager asked. Against Nantes, he scored his first goal after four minutes. Then just before half-time, he steered Bernardo's incredible cross past the keeper.

Goooooooooooooooooooooaaaaaaaaaaaaaaaalllllllllllll lllllllllllllllll!!!!!!!!!!!!!!!!!!!

Kylian roared up at the crowd, pumping both fists. It was another special occasion for him. He had just scored his tenth Ligue 1 goal and he was the youngest player to have achieved that for thirty years. Forget the 'New Henry' nickname – Kylian was on track to become the best player ever!

'Are you surprised by how well Mbappé's playing?' the journalists asked Jardim. Suddenly, everyone wanted to know everything about France's latest wonderkid.

'No, not at all,' the Monaco manager replied. 'I've worked with him every day since he was seventeen. We know that he's a player of great quality with a spectacular future ahead of him.'

Yes, what a season Kylian was having! His record on the pitch was remarkable – a goal or an assist every sixty minutes. But would he be able to keep that up? Of course he could! He was feeling as confident as ever.

CHAPTER 13

MAGIC VS MANCHESTER CITY

Scoring goals for fun in France was one thing, but what about in Europe? The Champions League was the greatest club competition in the world. That was where a star could become a *super*star. Messi, Cristiano, Neymar Jr… could Kylian be next?

In the group stage, however, he only played twenty-five minutes of Monaco's six matches: thirteen minutes against Bayer Leverkusen and twelve minutes against CSKA Moscow; it just wasn't enough time to shine.

'I'm quick, but I'm not that quick!' Kylian joked with Jirés.

But that was all before he became a hat-trick hero.

By the time the Round of 16 started in February 2017, he was one half of Monaco's star strikeforce – Radamel and Kylian. Would Jardim finally give him his first Champions League start, away at Pep Guardiola's Manchester City?

Yes! There was his name and shirt number on the teamsheet – 'MBAPPÉ 29'. Kylian wanted to run a victory lap around the training pitch but instead, he played it cool. Starting in the Champions League at the age of eighteen? No big deal!

'Thanks boss, I won't let you down,' Kylian said with a serious look on his young face.

Over 53,000 fans packed into Manchester City's Etihad Stadium for the biggest game of the season so far. As the teams walked out of the tunnel and onto the pitch, Kylian's whole body was buzzing. Both sets of supporters were making so much noise! It was even better than he'd imagined in his childhood dreams.

'Attack down the right wing whenever you can,' Radamel told Kylian as they waited to take the kick-off together. 'Fernandinho's a midfielder, not a left-back!'

'Will do!'

It was City who scored first, but Monaco kept fighting. They weren't the best team in defence but they were awesome in attack. Fabinho crossed to the back post and there was Radamel with a brilliant diving header. 1–1!

It was an end-to-end game, full of exciting football. The Manchester City defence couldn't handle Kylian's pace and movement. Radamel flicked the ball on and he sprinted past Yaya Touré and Nicolás Otamendi...

'Keep calm,' Kylian told himself.

He didn't want to waste it by shooting wildly, but unfortunately, that's exactly what he did.

'Hahahaha!' the City fans laughed, as the ball flew high and wide of the goal.

Kylian puffed out his cheeks. What a chance! He had to do better next time. He soon got a second chance. As Fabinho played the pass, Kylian raced into the penalty area, between the City centre-backs. The ball bounced up nicely for him to strike but Kylian didn't rush his finish this time. He slowed down and picked his spot – top corner. 2–1!

Goooooooooooooooooooaaaaaaaaaaaaaaaalllllllllll llllllllllllll!!!!!!!!!!!!!!!!!!!!

Kylian threw his arms out wide and then slid across the grass on his knees. 'Yesss!' he screamed. He had scored his first Champions League goal, and it was one of his best. Had he broken another record? No, not this time. He was only the second youngest Frenchman to score in the Champions League – Karim Benzema had been three months younger. Never mind!

'What a shot, *Casse-bonbon!*' Benjamin Mendy cheered. That was his new nickname for Kylian. It was the French for 'pain in the neck'.

From then, Monaco's night should have got even better. Radamel missed a penalty and Kylian missed another good chance. But instead, City pulled off an amazing comeback to win the first leg 5–3.

'I know you're disappointed,' Jardim told his players in the dressing room, 'but those away goals could be really important. Now, we have to go and win the second leg at home!'

'Yeah!' they all cheered together. Their team spirit was so strong.

Kylian had never heard such noise at the Stade Louis II. In one stand, the fans formed a wall of red and white.

'Monaco! Monaco! Monaco!' they chanted all night long.

Out on the pitch, the players did them proud. Kylian got his first chance in the sixth minute, but City's keeper made a good save.

'So close!' he groaned with his hands on his head. Still, it was a good sign...

Two minutes later, Bernardo crossed from the left and Kylian stuck out his right boot. Nutmeg! He poked the ball through the keeper's legs and into the net. 5–4!

Gooooooooooooooooooooaaaaaaaaaaaaaaaaaalllllllllll llllllllllllllll!!!!!!!!!!!!!!!!!!!

Kylian hardly gave himself time to celebrate his second Champions League goal. 'Let's go!' he called out, beckoning his teammates to follow him back to the halfway line. They had more work to do.

That early goal gave Monaco lots of confidence. Soon, Benjamin crossed to Fabinho – 5–5! Kylian ran over to high-five the goalscorer.

'We're almost there!' he screamed.

However, when Leroy Sané scored for City, Monaco needed to get another goal, or they were out. They could do it; Kylian never stopped believing. With fifteen minutes to go, Fabinho won a free kick on the right wing. Thomas curled the ball into the box and Tiémoué headed it in. 6–6!   The whole Monaco team chased after their hero.

They would qualify on the 'away goals' rule. An away goal victory was a close as a Champions League tie could be, but Kylian didn't care.'Quarter-finals, here we come!' he yelled to the fans above.

At the final whistle, the players ran towards each other for a big team hug. Against the odds, they had beaten Manchester City!

It was a famous win for the club, and a famous night for Kylian too. He had just scored two goals in two games against one of the best teams in the world.

He was no longer just the talk of France; Kylian was now the talk of the whole football world.

CHAPTER 14

CHAMPIONS OF FRANCE

Kylian's first Champions League adventure didn't end there. He was becoming more and more consistent as the competition went on. In the quarter-finals against Borussia Dortmund in April 2017, he was Monaco's main man again.

Away in Germany, Thomas crossed and Kylian bundled the ball in. 1–0!

Then in the second half, he stole the ball off the Dortmund defence, steadied himself and slammed a shot into the top corner. 3–1!

Goooooooooooooooooooooaaaaaaaaaaaaaaaaallllllllllll lllllllllllllllll!!!!!!!!!!!!!!!!!!!!

It was time for Kylian's new celebration pose. He

slid on his knees, folded his arms across his chest, and tried to look as cool as possible. He had his younger brother to thank for the pose. That's what Ethan did whenever he beat Kylian at FIFA.

'You can't keep copying Ronaldo when you score,' Ethan told him. 'You're a superstar now. You need a move of your own!'

Kylian had to use his awesome new celebration pose again in the second leg against Dortmund. It was his fifth goal in four games – he was officially on fire! He scored one more in the semi-final against Juventus but that's where his amazing first Champions League journey came to an end – Monaco lost 4–1 on aggregate.

'I'll be back,' Kylian promised himself, 'and one day, I'm going to lift that trophy!'

He had to move on quickly, though, because Monaco had other prizes to fight for. PSG beat them in the French Cup semi-final and the League Cup final, but their Ligue 1 title dream was still alive.

Game after game, Monaco kept on winning because Kylian kept on scoring. He got the opening goal to beat Bordeaux, and then two more to conquer Caen. His composure was incredible.

'I wish all young players were as mature as you,' Radamel joked in training. 'You're got more sense than Benjamin and Tiémoué put together!'

But every time Monaco won, PSG won too. PSG were still only three points behind in second place. Every weekend, the pressure was on to perform well. One slip-up and the title race could be wide open again.

Monaco's trip to Lyon would be particularly tough. Lyon were fourth in Ligue 1 and they had a talented team featuring Memphis Depay, Mathieu Valbuena, and Kylian's old Under-19 captain, Lucas.

'Come on, six more wins and the title's ours!' Jardim reminded his players before kick-off.

Kylian was determined. They couldn't end their sensational season without a single trophy!

Against Lyon, Radamel scored first but they knew that one goal wouldn't be enough. Monaco needed a second to make things safe. Just before half-time, Bernardo found Kylian in space on the left wing.

Uh oh, Lyon were in big trouble. Kylian licked his

lips and raced forward at speed. He was so dangerous on the dribble. Lyon's centre-back Mouctar Diakhaby backed away and backed away, too scared to attempt a tackle.

Stepover to the left, a little hop, and then GO!

To finish, Kylian lifted the ball over the diving keeper and into the back of the net.

Goooooooooooooooooooaaaaaaaaaaaaaaaaaalllllllllllll llllllllllllllll!!!!!!!!!!!!!!!!!!!!

2–0! Kylian skidded over to the corner flag, with his arms firmly folded. The fans were going wild up above, but not him. He stayed as cool as ever.

'What a hero!' Bernardo cried out when he caught up with his teammate.

Kylian nodded his head as he got back to his feet. Yes, he was a hero – Monaco's hero. And with his help, they were going to win that league title, no matter what.

'Five more wins!' Jardin urged his players on.

The next weekend, Monaco took on Toulouse on the Saturday. Again, Kylian's name was there on the teamsheet and again, it was there on the scoresheet too. There was just no stopping him, or his team. From 1–0 down, they fought back to win 3–1.

'We're nearly there!' Kylian shouted to the supporters at the final whistle.

That Monaco victory put the pressure back on PSG. Could they beat Nice on the Sunday? No, they lost 3–1!

'Two more wins!' Jardim told his players before their match against Lille. The finish line was in sight!

Just before half-time, Kylian found himself one-on-one with the left-back on the edge of the penalty area. Uh oh, Lille were in big trouble. Kylian twisted and turned, one way and then the other, with his fancy feet flashing. First right, then left, then right again. ZOOM! With a burst of speed, Kylian dribbled through and crossed to Bernardo. 2–0!

'Thanks, Kylian!'

In the second half, Thomas chipped a clever pass over the top to Kylian. He could have taken a touch to control it but no, he had a better idea. He could see Radamel waiting in the middle, so he crossed it first time on the volley. 3–0!

'Thanks, Kylian!'

One more win – that was all Monaco needed now. There was a tense atmosphere at the Stade Louis II ahead of their match against Saint-Étienne. Could they claim the title in front of their home crowd? It would be the perfect way to win it.

Monaco! Monaco! Monaco!

Kylian was desperate to be his team's hero yet again. He hit a powerful early strike but the Saint-Étienne goalkeeper made a good save.

'What a chance!' Kylian sighed heavily. Next time, he had to score.

Radamel played the perfect pass and Kylian was off, sprinting straight past the Saint-Étienne defence. Now he just had the keeper to beat. He looked up and picked his spot – bottom corner. He pulled back his right foot and...

...DUMMY!

As the goalkeeper dived, Kylian dribbled around him and passed the ball into the empty net. 1–0!

Goooooooooooooooooooooaaaaaaaaaaaaaaaaalllllllllllll llllllllllllllll!!!!!!!!!!!!!!!!!!!!!

'Phew, I thought you were going to miss that!' Radamel said as they celebrated.

Kylian just laughed. 'Me? Never!'

Would one goal be enough? No, Monaco needed a second to make things safe but it didn't arrive until the last minute. Thomas crossed to Valère. 2–0!

By then, Kylian had been substituted, so he stood there clapping and cheering on the sidelines. Why wasn't the referee blowing the final whistle yet? He was ready to run back on for the big title celebrations.

The party had already started in the stadium. The fans waved their red-and-white flags and sang at the top of their voices:

Campiones, Campiones, Olé! Olé! Olé!

Finally, the match was over, and so was Monaco's seventeen-year wait. They were the Champions of France again!

Campiones, Campiones, Olé! Olé! Olé!

It was a moment that Kylian would never forget for as long as he lived. He was soon at the centre of the big team hug on the pitch. Monaco's superstars moved around the pitch together –

Radamel, Fabinho, Benjamin, Bernardo, Boschilia, Tiémoué, Thomas, Valère, and, of course, Kylian – all applauding the fans.

What an important part he had played in his first full season – 15 goals and 11 assists! And that was only in Ligue 1, where he was the clear winner of the Young Player of the Year award.

In total, Kylian had finished with 26 goals and 14 assists. All that, and he was still only eighteen years old. His stats were way better than Messi or Cristiano at that age. At this rate, Kylian would achieve his dream of becoming the best footballer ever.

Once they had collected their winners' medals and lifted the Ligue 1 trophy, the Monaco players returned to the dressing room to get ready for a big night out.

'Are you coming, mate?' Tiémoué asked.

Kylian shook his head. 'Sorry, I'm tired. I'm going to go home, but have fun!'

For him, the Ligue 1 title was just another goal achieved. The next day, he would move straight on to his next two targets – the Champions League and the World Cup.

CHAPTER 15

FRANCE'S NEW FLAIR PLAYER

'Mbappé for France!'

The Monaco fans had been calling for him ever since the start of the 2016–17 season. 'Yes, he's still young, but look how amazing he is *already*. He could win the World Cup for us in a few years!'

Didier Deschamps, the national team coach, wasn't so sure. What was the rush? At that stage, Kylian was still only seventeen. So, he didn't make the senior France squad for the qualifiers against Belarus in September 2016, or against Bulgaria and the Netherlands in October, or against Sweden in November either.

But by March 2017, Kylian had forced Deschamps to change his mind. How could he say no to

Monaco's young hat-trick hero, especially after his magic against Manchester City? France were crying out for a flair player like that.

'Who knows, maybe we wouldn't have lost the Euro 2016 final if we'd had Mbappé in the team!' his fans argued.

Kylian had watched that final on TV in Germany with the national Under-19s squad. It was France vs Portugal, his nation vs his hero, Cristiano. France were the clear favourites to win. They were playing at home at the Stade de France and their attacking trio – Olivier Giroud, Antoine Griezmann and Dimitri Payet – had looked awesome all tournament.

'Allez la France! Allez la France!' Kylian and his teammates cheered.

In the final, however, France's forwards just could not find a way past the Portugal defence. When Dimitri got injured, Deschamps brought on Kingsley Coman, but he couldn't change the game either. Neither could André-Pierre Gignac or Anthony Martial. In the end, it was Portugal's Eder who scored the winning goal.

'How on earth did we lose that?' France's junior stars asked each other in disbelief. Back home in Paris, their senior stars were asking themselves the exact same question.

'I could have changed that game' – Kylian didn't say it out loud but that's what he was thinking. He had the speed, the skill *and* the confidence. Two weeks later, he helped France to win the Under-19 Euros. If only...

But now, nine months after that Euro 2016 final, Kylian was about to skip straight to the French senior team. Deschamps named his squad for the World Cup qualifier against Luxembourg:

Hugo Lloris, Laurent Koscielny, Paul Pogba, Antoine Griezmann, Olivier Giroud, Dimitri Payet...

There were lots of older, experienced players on the list but there was also a new young star:

...Kylian Mbappé.

'Congratulations!' his proud parents cried down the phone.

'Well done, you deserve it!' his Monaco manager told him.

'You and me, *Casse-bonbon*,' his club teammate Benjamin cheered happily. It was his first call-up too. 'Let's do this!'

What an honour! Being called up to the national team was a dream come true for Kylian, but it wouldn't mean much unless he actually played. If he came on, would he become France's youngest-ever international? He loved breaking records. But no, it turned out Maryan Wisnieski had been thirty-three days younger when he made his debut in 1955!

Still, Kylian was desperate to play against Luxembourg. Hopefully, if France were winning comfortably, he would get his chance.

Djibril Sidibé cut the ball back to Olivier. 1–0!

On the sidelines, Kylian punched the air. They were off to a good start but five minutes later, Luxembourg won a penalty. 1–1!

'Maybe they'll need me to come on and change the game,' Kylian thought, trying to think positively.

But no, Antoine scored from the spot. 2–1!

Then Benjamin crossed to Olivier. 3–1!

Was that game over? Deschamps decided to take

off Dimitri and replace him with… Kylian! He was already warmed up and raring to go.

'Use your speed to attack down the left,' his manager told him.

Sure thing! Wearing the white 'Number 12' shirt, Kylian raced out onto the field. He didn't think about the fact that he was making his senior France debut, or about his talented new teammates. All he thought about was getting on the ball as quickly as possible. How much magic could he create in the last fifteen minutes?

Plenty! Ousmane Dembélé curled a great pass to Kylian as he ran down the wing. Uh oh, Luxembourg were in big trouble. He stayed calm and hit a powerful shot with his left foot, but the goalkeeper managed to tip it over the bar.

So close! Kylian winced. It was nearly the perfect start to his senior international career.

He didn't get another chance to shoot, but he did get the chance to show off his full range of fancy skills and stepovers.

'Hurray!' the France fans cheered. They loved their new flair player.

ZOOM! Kylian sprinted straight past Luxembourg's right-back and crossed the ball into the box. Olivier stretched out his right foot, but he couldn't quite reach it.

So close! Kylian winced again. He had nearly helped Olivier to get his hat-trick.

'Great ball!' the striker shouted, giving him a thumbs-up.

Kylian soon ran out of time but three days later, Deschamps picked him to start in the friendly match against Spain at the Stade de France in Paris.

'Thanks boss, you won't regret it!'

In his hometown, Kylian would get to play sixty, seventy, maybe even ninety minutes of football! He couldn't wait. In the tunnel, he looked as relaxed as ever, but once the match kicked off, he was fully focused on winning and scoring.

A cross came in from the left, and Kylian cleverly flicked it goalwards… but David De Gea made a super save!

So close! For a moment, Kylian stood there with his head in his hands, but then he chased back to get the ball again. He still had plenty of time left.

Kylian certainly didn't look like the new kid on the block. He was linking up really well with Antoine, playing one-twos all over the pitch. Was this the future of France's attack? The fans hoped so.

At half-time, Gerard Piqué even asked to swap shirts with him. What? The Barcelona centre-back had won pretty much everything there was to win in football – the World Cup, the Euros, the Champions League, the Spanish League. But now, Piqué wanted Kylian's shirt!

'Sure,' he replied, sounding as cool as ever.

After sixty-five minutes, Deschamps replaced Kylian with Olivier. At that point, the score was 0–0, but soon, France were 2–0 down.

'That's what happens when you take Mbappé off!' his supporters argued.

Oh well, Kylian's first international goal and assist would have to wait a little longer. That was okay; he would have plenty more chances to impress. At the age of eighteen, he was only just getting started.

CHAPTER 16

WHICH CLUB TO CHOOSE? PART II

After winning the Ligue 1 title for the 2016–17 season, what was next for Monaco? Would they grow stronger, or was it a one-off success? Would they be able to buy even better players, or would they lose their superstars? Unfortunately, it was a story with a sad ending.

Bernardo Silva was the first to go, moving to Manchester City in May 2017.

'I'm going to miss playing with you!' Kylian admitted as they said their goodbyes.

Next, Nabil Dirar went to Fenerbahçe, and Valère Germain went to Marseille, while in July, Tiémoué Bakayoko left to join Chelsea.

'Don't go!' Kylian begged his friend.

Then, to make matters even worse, Benjamin Mendy moved to Manchester City as well.

'No, not you too! Why is everyone abandoning me?' Kylian complained.

At this rate, it would just be him, Radamel Falcao, Thomas Lemar and Fabinho left! Monaco had no chance against the power of PSG, especially when their rivals signed Neymar Jr from Barcelona for £200 million.

'They'll win the league easily now!' Kylian thought to himself.

Was it time for Kylian to move on too? He loved his club but he wanted to win the top trophies. That didn't look very likely to happen at Monaco.

Kylian thought long and hard about what was best for his career. He was one of the top players in the world now, and the big clubs were queuing up to buy him once again. But which one would he choose?

Arsenal? Arsène Wenger had been trying to sign him for years but The Gunners weren't even in the Champions League anymore. Kylian had his eyes firmly fixed on that prize.

Liverpool? Kylian had an exciting conversation with their manager, Jürgen Klopp, but unfortunately, the club couldn't afford to buy him.

Manchester City? That was a possibility. Money wasn't a problem for them, and Kylian had really impressed Pep Guardiola with his Champions League magic.

'Come join our exciting project,' the City manager tried to persuade Kylian. 'Think about it – you, Sergio Agüero, Leroy Sané and Gabriel Jesus in attack, with Kevin De Bruyne and David Silva in midfield. We would win every trophy there is!'

Working with Guardiola would be an amazing experience, but playing in the Premier League? Kylian wasn't so sure about that – what other options did he have?

Barcelona? With Neymar Jr gone, was there a gap next to Lionel Messi and Luis Suárez? No, they eventually decided to sign his France teammate Ousmane Dembélé instead.

Real Madrid? How cool would it be if Kylian

and Cristiano could play together in the same star strikeforce. They would be unstoppable! Real's manager, Zidane, loved that idea and so did the club president, Florentino Pérez. He met with the Monaco chairman, Dmitry Rybolovlev, to agree a deal.

'We want £170 million for Mbappé.'

'We'll offer £130 million, plus an extra £25 million in bonuses.'

Pérez left France, feeling very confident. The deal wasn't quite done yet, but it seemed like only a matter of time before Real got their new Galáctico signing.

Kylian was excited too. He had dreamed of playing for the club ever since his first trip to Madrid for his fourteenth birthday – plus Real had just won the Spanish League *and* the Champions League.

'Don't get your hopes up yet,' his dad told him. 'There's still a lot to work out before you get to wear that famous white shirt!'

Wilfried was also now Kylian's agent and he travelled to Spain to meet with Pérez and the club directors. There was one important issue that he wanted to discuss: Kylian's role in the Real team. After all, he wasn't going to move to Madrid to just sit on the Bernabéu bench.

'So, where will my son fit into the starting line-up?' Wilfried asked.

It was a good question. Real already had their star strikeforce, 'BBC' - Karim Benzema, Gareth Bale and Cristiano. They also had two young talents waiting in the wings: Isco and Marco Asensio. Did they really have space for another wonderkid?

'Don't worry, we'll make room for Kylian,' Pérez promised.

However, by the middle of August, nothing had changed. Real still had all of their attacking stars.

'Sorry, son,' Wilfried said. 'I don't think that's a good move for you right now.'

There was one last option left – Kylian's hometown club, PSG. They were desperate for him to become the third member of their amazing new all-star attack. Forget Barcelona's 'MSN' or Real Madrid's 'BBC'; PSG were aiming for 'MCN': Kylian Mbappé, Edinson Cavani and Neymar Jr.

'With the three of you, we believe that we can win the Champions League,' PSG's manager, Unai Emery, declared confidently.

That was exactly what Kylian wanted to hear! Not only were PSG offering him regular first-team football, but they were building a top-quality team to take on Barcelona and Real Madrid. He would even get to play with one of his heroes, Neymar Jr! Kylian used to play as PSG on FIFA so that he could use the Brazilian to beat his brother Ethan.

'I'm in!' Kylian told his dad.

There was one big problem, though. Would Monaco really sell Kylian to their biggest Ligue 1 rivals? They didn't want to say yes, but PSG's offer was too good to say no to – the full asking price of £170 million. It wouldn't be paid straight away because PSG had already spent so much money on Neymar Jr, but they would take Kylian on loan for one year and then pay the full amount the next season.

Monaco could see that Kylian's mind was made up. He wanted to return home to Paris and there was no point trying to stop him. On 31 August 2017, the deal was done. Suddenly, his face was seen all over his city.

'Welcome Kylian,' said one poster.

'Paris loves Mbappé,' said another.

Another just showed his number – 29, the same shirt that he had worn at Monaco.

Kylian had already been famous but now that he was a PSG player, he was super-famous. Every time he tried to leave his house, fans surrounded him in seconds, asking for photos and autographs. It was crazy; he couldn't go anywhere anymore!

Oh well, Kylian would just have to get used to all the extra attention. For now, though, he was fully focused on football.

'I really wanted to be part of the club's project,' he had told the media. 'It's one of the most ambitious in Europe.'

It was time for PSG's stars to prove themselves. Kylian, Edinson and Neymar Jr – they were about to take on their greatest challenge together.

CHAPTER 17

OFF THE MARK FOR FRANCE

Before making his debut for his new club, PSG, however, Kylian had two more games to play for his country. A shock defeat to Sweden meant that France really needed two wins in their World Cup qualifiers against The Netherlands and Luxembourg.

'Let's do this!' Kylian told his old Monaco teammate, Thomas Lemar.

Kylian had only just signed for PSG but luckily, he didn't have far to travel for the first game. The Stade de France was only an hour's bus ride across Paris from the PSG ground at Parc des Princes. He was really looking forward to representing his country again. He was now the second most expensive player

in the world, but his international record still stood
at four games and zero goals. He had failed to score
in twenty minutes against Sweden, or in ninety-five
minutes against England.

'I've really got to do something about that,' Kylian
told his teammates, with that serious look on his
face.

The Netherlands team weren't as strong as they
used to be but Didier Deschamps wasn't taking
any risks. The France manager stuck with his usual
formation – Kingsley Coman and Thomas Lemar
on the wings, with Antoine Griezmann and Olivier
Giroud up front. That left Kylian waiting impatiently
on the bench again.

'Allez les Bleus!' he mumbled, shaking his restless
legs. How long would he have to wait?

Antoine played a great one-two with Olivier and
then nutmegged the keeper. 1–0!

Kylian slumped a little further down in his seat. If
France's strikers kept playing like that, he wouldn't
be needed at all! However, sixty minutes went by
before Thomas made it 2–0 with a superstrike.

'Bring me on, bring me on!'

Kylian looked over at Deschamps. Was the manager ready to make a change? Yes, he was – and a few minutes later, Kylian finally came on to replace Olivier.

'Hurray, it's Mbappé!' the fans cheered.

Right – Kylian had twenty minutes to score his first goal for France. That seemed like plenty of time but it would soon fly by if he didn't take his chances...

He dribbled through the tired Dutch defence but the keeper saved his shot.

'Hey, look up!' Antoine shouted angrily, standing in lots of space.

'Sorry!'

The next time Kylian ran forward, Kylian did pass the ball to Djibril Sidibé, but he asked for it straight back.

'Now!' he cried out, sprinting into the penalty area.

Djibril's pass was perfect and so was Kylian's finish. This time, the keeper had no chance.

Goooooooooooooooooooaaaaaaaaaaaaaaaaalllllllllll llllllllllllllll!!!!!!!!!!!!!!!!!!!!

Kylian raced behind the goal with his arms and mouth wide open. At last, he was off the mark for France! It was another target achieved before his nineteenth birthday.

Kylian wasn't his country's youngest scorer ever but he was their youngest scorer for fifty-four years. That was a long, long time, and a good reason to crack out his trademark celebration pose. He stopped, folded his arms across his chest, and stood there looking as cool as possible.

'You're allowed to be excited, you know!' Thomas laughed.

The France players all came over to congratulate him – Djibril, Paul Pogba, Alexandre Lacazette. Kylian really felt part of the team now.

'Excellent victory yesterday,' he wrote on Instagram, next to a picture of his celebration.

At that stage, he was wearing France's Number 20 shirt, but hopefully that wouldn't be the case for long. Antoine wore Number 7 and Olivier wore

Number 9. Kylian had his eyes on Number 10. That shirt had belonged to Zidane, France's last World Cup hero.

A deadly display in the next match would surely do the trick. Kylian couldn't wait to start in attack with Antoine and Olivier against a nation ranked 136th in the world. Now that he was off the mark, the goals would surely start to flow. Uh oh, Luxembourg were in big trouble…

But no, it turned out to be a really frustrating night for France. They had so many chances, but they couldn't score a single one! Their composure had completely disappeared.

Kylian pulled the ball back to Antoine but he blasted it high over the bar. MISSED!

He played a quick one-two with Antoine but a defender got in the way of his shot. BLOCKED!

Kylian danced through the Luxembourg defence but then fired straight at the goalkeeper. SAVED!

He threw his arms up in frustration. What was going wrong? Were they trying too hard, or not hard enough? Kylian couldn't tell. He showed off his full range of tricks, flicks and stepovers, but none of it was working. The score was still 0–0. After sixty minutes, Deschamps took Kylian off and put Kingsley on the right wing instead.

'You were unlucky not to score today,' his manager told him, 'but you've got to learn to take your chances.'

It was a harsh but very important lesson for Kylian. Deschamps had so many talented attackers to choose from: Antoine and Olivier, but also Ousmane, Kingsley, Alexandre, Dimitri Payet, Nabil Fekir, Florian Thauvin and Anthony Martial. The pressure was really on to perform.

Kylian had a £170 million price-tag at club level, but that didn't mean anything at international level. In order to achieve his target of playing at the 2018 World Cup, he still had a lot to prove. Deschamps knew that he could be a gamechanger off the bench, but was that the role he wanted? No, Kylian wanted that Number 10 shirt; he wanted to be France's flair player right from the start.

CHAPTER 18

MCN: THE EARLY DAYS

The PSG fans couldn't wait to see Kylian, and
'MCN', in action, and in September 2017 they got
their first opportunity. Uh oh, their first opponents
Metz were soon in big trouble.

After thirty minutes, Neymar Jr slipped the ball
through for his strike partners to chase. Kylian was
desperate to score on his debut, but he let Edinson
take the shot instead.

1– 0!

'Thanks!' the Uruguayan said, giving his
teammate a big hug.

'No problem!'

'MCN' were going to need to work together

to succeed. They were three superstars but they couldn't be selfish. There was no 'I' in 'team', and especially not in 'great team'.

So, who would score next – Kylian or Neymar Jr? In the second half, Kylian chipped the ball forward to the Brazilian. A defender cleared it but it bounced straight back to Kylian. *BANG!*

Goooooooooooooooooooooaaaaaaaaaaaaaaaaalllllllllll llllllllllllllll!!!!!!!!!!!!!!!!!!!

2–1! 'Yes!' Kylian screamed out, throwing his arms out wide. One game, one goal – Kylian was already off the mark at PSG.

Who would score next? Neymar Jr, of course! He dribbled through and found the bottom corner. 3–1!

Edinson and Kylian jogged over to congratulate the Brazilian. One goal each for all three of them – what a start for 'MCN'! The 2017–18 season was only just beginning, but the future looked very bright for PSG...

...Just as long as they remembered to work together. The following week they were 1–0 up against Lyon when Kylian won a penalty.

'Hurray!' the supporters cheered at first, but that soon turned to:

'BOOOOOOOOOOOOOOOOOOOOOO!'

Edinson had been the team's penalty taker for ages and he was the fans' favourite. But Neymar Jr was trying to steal the spot-kick instead.

'Who does he think he is?' the PSG supporters spat angrily. 'He's only just arrived and he already thinks he owns the place!'

Eventually, Neymar Jr walked away but the Brazilian clearly wasn't happy. To make matters worse, Edinson's penalty then struck the crossbar.

'Come on, we're meant to be a *team!*' Kylian told his strike partners, trying to act as the peacemaker.

'MCN' needed each other. When Neymar Jr missed the next match against Montpellier, 'M' and 'C' couldn't score without him. Kylian had one shot blocked, one shot saved, and one shot cleared off the goal line.

'What's wrong with me today?' he groaned, wiping the sweat off his forehead.

When 'MCN' were reunited a week later against

Bordeaux, they made up for that goalless draw against Montpellier.

Neymar Jr scored a free kick. 1–0!

Edinson poked home the Brazilian's pass. 2–0!

Kylian fluffed his shot but right-back Thomas Meunier scored instead. 3–0!

Edinson let Neymar Jr take the penalty. 4–1!

Julian Draxler volleyed in Kylian's cross. 5–1 at half-time!

The only thing missing was a Kylian goal. He had to get at least one! He vowed he wasn't leaving the pitch until he had added his name to the scoresheet.

Julian returned the favour to Kylian in the second half. Kylian ran on to his pass and picked his spot – far bottom corner. 6–1!

'Finally!' he said to himself with a smile. Kylian dedicated his goal to his injured friend, Benjamin Mendy. He held up two fingers on each hand to make '22', Benjamin's shirt number at Manchester City.

In the dressing room afterwards, manager Unai Emery praised the PSG players. 'See, look what you can achieve when you help each other!'

By the Christmas break, they were nine points clear of Kylian's old club Monaco at the top of the Ligue 1 table. They had won 16 of their 19 games, scoring 58 goals along the way. That included 19 for Edinson, 11 for Neymar Jr and 8 for Kylian.

He wasn't always the star of the show for PSG, but Kylian was the youngest by far and he was just happy to be helping his team out. Along with his eight goals, he also had seven assists. Those were very good numbers and besides, he was looking for club trophies, not individual awards. So far, he was cruising to his second French league title in a row.

He was also learning lots. He had only just turned nineteen and yet he was playing alongside Edinson and Neymar Jr, plus Ángel Di María, Dani Alves, Thiago Silva, Marco Verratti… the list went on and on! With such experienced and talented teammates, Kylian was improving all the time.

'Hey, you're a superstar too, you know!' Neymar Jr kept reminding him.

The Brazilian was six years older than Kylian, but

they got on really well. They were always laughing, joking and posing for Instagram photos together – on airplanes, on the training ground, on the pitch celebrating goals, even at awards ceremonies dressed in smart suits.

'Smile for the followers!'

Kylian was careful not to lose his football focus, though. He was the second most expensive player in the world and the new 'Golden Boy', the best young player in Europe. That was a lot to live up to. Plus, with Ángel playing well, he had to keep fighting for his starting spot. He came off the bench against Dijon with twenty-five minutes to go. Plenty of time to win back his place!

PSG were already winning 5–0, so Kylian could go out onto the Parc des Princes pitch and enjoy himself. With 'MCN' playing together again, the crowd expected more. They got more! Neymar Jr scored the sixth and Kylian scored the seventh.

'Goal time!' he roared, jumping into the Brazilian's arms.

After the match, Kylian posted an Instagram photo

with one arm around Edinson, 'The Matador', and one arm around Neymar Jr, 'Crack x 4'.

Now that they were a happy family, were 'MCN' unstoppable? Not quite. It was easy to forget that Kylian was still so young. It felt like he had been playing football forever! Most of the time, he seemed very mature but occasionally, he did act like the teenager that he was. He was growing up in public and that wasn't always easy.

In the League Cup semi-final against Rennes in January 2018, PSG were winning 3–0 when Kylian took out his frustration on Ismaïla Sarr. It was a silly late tackle and, in a flash, he was surrounded by angry opponents.

'What did you do that for?' they asked, pushing him back.

'Ref, that was reckless. Send him off!' they shouted.

Red card! Kylian walked off slowly, shaking his head and removing his gloves.

'A player did that to me last week and what did he get? Nothing, not even a yellow!' he muttered moodily.

Once he had calmed down, however, Kylian felt guilty and embarrassed. He had let his team down and left them to defend with ten men. What a stupid error! Rennes scored twice, but at least PSG held on for the victory. *Phew!*

'I'm really sorry, that won't happen again,' Kylian promised his manager and teammates. He had definitely learnt his lesson.

'Don't worry, we still won,' Edinson reassured him.

'We all make mistakes,' Neymar Jr comforted him. 'Just try not to make any against Real Madrid in the Champions League, okay?'

CHAPTER 19

KYLIAN VS CRISTIANO

That's right – in the Champions League Round of 16, it was Kylian's 'MCN' vs Cristiano's 'BBC'. At last, he would come face-to-face with his childhood hero on the football pitch. What an exciting encounter! What a fascinating fixture! PSG were cruising to the Ligue 1 title but were they strong enough to challenge Real Madrid, the European Champions?

So far, so good! In the group stage, in the autumn of 2017, PSG had already thrashed Celtic 5–0 and 7–1, and Anderlecht 4–0 and 5–0. That was twenty-one goals scored in only four games!

Kylian's favourite game, however, was the 3–0 win over German giants Bayern Munich. That night, at the Parc des Princes, 'MCN' had been simply unstoppable. In the very first minute of the match, Neymar Jr dribbled all the way across the penalty area and set up Dani Alves to strike it. 1–0!

Most of the time, Kylian had two Bayern defenders marking his every move. No problem! He used his strength and skill to hold the ball up until Edinson arrived. 2–0!

Again and again, Kylian created great chances for his strike partners. Edinson and Neymar Jr could have both had hat-tricks, but in the end, they got one goal each.

As Kylian went to cross the ball, Bayern's left-back David Alaba jumped up to make the block. Just kidding! Kylian rolled the ball across to his other foot instead.

'Hurray!' cheered the PSG fans of his sublime skill.

Kylian dribbled between Alaba and Niklas Süle, and this time, he did cross to Neymar Jr. 3–0!

What a night it had been for all three members of 'MCN'! Although Kylian hadn't scored himself, he had set up two goals against one of the best teams in the world. Now, it was time to take on Real Madrid.

The first leg was played away at the Bernabéu. The PSG players were feeling confident as their plane landed in Spain. They were top of Ligue 1, whereas Real Madrid were only third in La Liga. At their best, PSG knew that they could beat anyone, even the European Champions.

'This is it, guys, the match you've been waiting for!' Emery told his team in the dressing room. 'I need you to be fearless out there tonight.'

Kylian looked around at Neymar Jr, Edinson, Marco, Dani Alves, Thiago Silva – yes, they were all fired up and raring to go.

'Let's win this!' the team cheered together.

Kylian liked to think that he was one of the coolest guys around, but even he was shocked by the atmosphere in the stadium. As he walked out onto the pitch, it was like being surrounded by four walls of deafening noise. So that was what 80,000 fans sounded like. Wow!

Looking up, Kylian could see an enormous blue

banner, reading 'VAMOS REAL!' Yes, they were in for their toughest battle yet.

Cristiano took the first shot, but it was PSG who scored the first goal. Out on the right wing, Kylian turned and skipped brilliantly past Marcelo. As he sprinted forward, he had Edinson at the front post and Neymar Jr at the back post. Thanks to Edinson's clever dummy, Kylian's cross ran all the way through to the Brazilian. His shot was blocked but eventually, the ball fell to Adrien Rabiot. 1–0!

'Yes!' Kylian yelled out, pumping his fists. He was playing his part for PSG.

The Bernabéu was stunned into silence, and Cristiano was furious. It wasn't a good idea to anger 'The Beast'. There was no way he was going to let his team lose like that. He scored a penalty just before half-time and then a tap-in with ten minutes to go. The first leg finished Real Madrid 3 PSG 1.

Kylian was hurting as he hugged Cristiano. 'Well played,' was all he could say to his hero.

In fact, 3–1 didn't feel like a fair result at all. PSG had wasted some excellent chances. On the flight home, Kylian couldn't help thinking back to the ones he had missed: the shot that flew straight at the keeper, the cross that he couldn't quite reach.

'Hey, it's not over yet,' Neymar Jr reassured him. 'We can beat them at home!'

The two teams reconvened in Paris the following month, March 2018. As the teams walked out of the tunnel, the Parc des Princes was covered in blue, white and red. They were the colours of PSG, and the colours of France. This time, Kylian looked up at an enormous red banner, reading, 'ENSEMBLE, ON VA LE FAIRE!'

'Together, we will do it.' That's right – teamwork was going to be a key part of PSG's gameplan. They had eleven players out there on the pitch; not just 'MCN'.

Real could have gone 4– or 5–1 up, but with half-time approaching, it was still 3–1. Neymar Jr slipped a great pass through to Kylian. Could he be the PSG hero? The angle was tight but he decided to shoot anyway… saved by the keeper!

'Why didn't you cross it?' Edinson screamed. He

was waiting in the middle for an easy finish.

Kylian put his head in his hands. He had definitely made the wrong decision. 'Sorry!'

It was exactly as Deschamps had told him after France's draw with Luxembourg – Kylian had to learn to take his chances. If he didn't, his team wouldn't win. Early in the second half, Cristiano scored a header: 4–1 to Real!

Kylian's heart sank. That was pretty much game over. Or was it? Edinson did pull one goal back, but that was nowhere near enough. They were out of the Champions League.

PSG 2 Real Madrid 5,

Kylian 0 Cristiano 3.

'Hey, this time we failed,' Thiago Silva comforted Kylian at the final whistle, 'but next time, we'll succeed, okay?'

Kylian nodded but in his head, he was still asking himself, 'Why didn't I square it to Edinson?'

It would take him a few days to get over the disappointment, but thankfully Kylian had other targets to aim for. PSG could still win another French treble.

CHAPTER 20

TROPHY TIME

PSG had won their first trophy of the 2017–18 season way back in July 2017 – the Champions Trophy. Kylian had played that day, but for the losing team, Monaco.

'That one doesn't count!' he decided, and Neymar Jr agreed. He hadn't played in the match at all. In fact, Edinson had been the only member of the 'MCN' trio at PSG at that point.

So, the team really needed to win some new trophies to make Kylian and Neymar Jr happy. PSG were out of the Champions League, but they were top of Ligue 1, through to the semi-finals of the French Cup, and through to the final of the League Cup.

Kylian planned to make the League Cup his PSG Trophy Number One. To lift it, however, he would have to beat his old club, Monaco. In the days before the final, in March 2018, there was lots of friendly banter between Kylian and his old teammates, Radamel, Fabinho and Thomas.

'MCN are coming for you!'

'Ha ha, we're not scared of your three-man team!'

'Yeah, enjoy your runners-up medal, mate!'

When the two teams had previously met in Ligue 1, Kylian played one of his worst games of the season. PSG won but he missed so many chances. This time, he was going to come back to haunt Monaco. With Neymar Jr out injured, the pressure was really on. He had to perform well.

In the eighth minute of the final, Kylian got the ball with his back to goal. He spun quickly and then ZOOM! he was off, dancing his way past Youri Tielemans…

then Jemerson…

then Fabinho…

until finally Kamil Glik fouled him.

'Hey!' Kylian cried out as he got back to his feet. 'That's a penalty. Check the VAR!'

The referee waited for the video assistant's verdict… *Penalty!* Edinson stepped up and scored. 1–0!

'Yes!' Kylian cheered, throwing both arms up in the air.

He was only just getting started. Soon, Kylian was on the ball again just outside his own box, and he raced forward on the counter-attack. His pace was so explosive that no-one could catch him. Just before the halfway line, Kylian looked up and spotted Ángel in space on the left. His pass was perfect. 2–0!

In the second half, Kylian dribbled towards goal again and this time, he poked a pass through to Edinson. 3–0!

Kylian was desperate to score a goal of his own, but a hat-trick of assists would definitely do. At the final whistle, he punched the air and then hugged his old teammates.

'Man, you tore us apart today!' Fabinho admitted.

Kylian smiled, 'Sorry, your messages just spurred me on!'

Instead of winner's medals, the PSG players got their own small versions of the League Cup.

'Well I know what I'm drinking out of tonight!' Dani Alves joked.

As he celebrated up on the stage, Kylian had his hands full. Not only was he holding a mini League Cup, but he also was also holding the Man of the Match award. As a big basketball fan, Kylian declared himself the 'MVP' on social media – the Most Valuable Player. What a night!

'Hurray!' he cried out, when captain Thiago Silva lifted the big gold trophy.

The next day, Kylian was already asking, 'Right, what's next?' His hunger was never satisfied.

Kylian's PSG Trophy Number Two would be the Ligue 1 title. They were just far too good for the rest of France. They had only lost two league games all season! The PSG squad was so full of stars that they didn't even miss Neymar Jr that much.

Kylian scored one goal with his left foot against

Metz, and then two goals with his right foot against Angers.

'We're nearly there!' he shouted as he celebrated with Edinson and left-back Layvin Kurzawa.

By mid-April, PSG were fourteen points clear at the top of the table. One more win would be enough to claim the title and who were their next opponents? Monaco!

Kylian was desperate to destroy his old club again but unfortunately, Emery picked Edinson, Ángel and Javier Pastore in attack instead. What? No way!

'Sorry, but we've got the French Cup semi-final coming up on Wednesday,' his manager explained to him. 'I need you fighting fit for that.'

Fine! Kylian sat grumpily with the other subs as his teammates scored goal after goal without him. By half-time, they were winning 4–1! He was so bored and frustrated that he started banging his head against the bench seat in front.

'This is torture!' he muttered.

Still, he joined in with the team celebrations at

the final whistle. 'CHAMPION LIGUE 1!' he posted on Instagram with a picture of all the PSG players.

The next day, he was already asking, 'Right, what's next?'

The answer – the French Cup, the final part of PSG's treble! After his rest against Monaco, Kylian was determined to be the star of the show in the semi-final. Uh oh, Caen were in big trouble.

Ángel passed it through to Edinson, who crossed to Kylian. 1–0!

Goooooooooooooooooooooaaaaaaaaaaaaaaaaalllllllllll llllllllllllllll!!!!!!!!!!!!!!!!!!!!

What a great team goal! Kylian leapt into Edinson's arms and punched the air. 'Come on!' he shouted.

Caen equalised just before half-time but PSG's amazing attackers weren't worried. They always believed that they could score another goal.

Ángel backheeled it to Edinson, who crossed to... Kylian again. 2–1!

They celebrated in the same way, except this time, Ángel jumped up on Kylian's back.

'We need a new name for the three of us,' the Argentine suggested. 'DMC?'

Edinson shook his head, and said, 'CMD.'

It was the MVP's turn to disagree. 'No way,' said Kylian, 'it's got to be MCD!'

Thanks to Kylian's twenty-first goal of the season, PSG were through to the French Cup final. Their opponents would be Les Herbiers.

'Who?' a lot of the PSG players and fans asked.

Even Kylian didn't know much about them, and he was the biggest football fan in France! However, he did know everything that he needed to know – PSG were going to beat them!

'Don't underestimate Les Herbiers today,' Emery warned his players before kick-off at the Stade de France. 'They will be so fired up for this!'

But so was Kylian. He really wanted his PSG Trophy Number Three. He was a hat-trick hero, after all.

In the first ten minutes, PSG hit the post twice – first Giovani Lo Celso, and then Kylian.

'How did that not go in?' he groaned, throwing his arms up in frustration.

Ángel headed over the bar and then Giovani clipped the post again! What was going on?

'Be patient,' Edinson told his teammates. 'We'll score soon.'

Giovani was third-time lucky. As he dribbled forward, Kylian made a clever run to create space for him. From the edge of the area, Giovani curled a shot into the bottom corner. 1–0!

'Finally!' Kylian said to himself.

His frustrations, however, continued in the second-half. Kylian thought he had made it 2–0, but no, the goal was disallowed for handball.

'Never, ref!' he protested but it was no use.

Luckily, Edinson soon scored a penalty to secure the win.

'Well done, guys!' Neymar Jr cheered. The Brazilian was still not fit enough to play in the final, but he was back in Paris and proudly wearing the PSG shirt.

'Let me hold it!' Neymar Jr begged as they paraded the French Cup trophy in front of the fans.

Kylian laughed and let his friend hold one of the

handles. Only one, though – he refused to let go of the whole trophy!

That was the end of Kylian's successful first season at PSG – twenty-one goals, fifteen assists and three trophies. A few days later, however, he posed with the four trophies that the club had won, holding up four fingers for the camera.

'You liar, you lost that Champions Trophy final!' Thiago Silva reminded Kylian with a big grin on his face. 'Or were you playing badly on purpose?'

CHAPTER 21

READY FOR RUSSIA

Although the 2017–18 club season was now over, Kylian still had a busy summer ahead of him. Instead of chilling out on a sunny beach somewhere, he would be playing for France at the 2018 World Cup. Hopefully…

Deschamps had so many amazing players to choose from, and only twenty-three of them would go to Russia. Would 'Mbappé' be one of the names that didn't make the list? Kylian would be so disappointed. He had dreamt of playing at a World Cup ever since watching Henry and Zidane back in 2006. It was the tournament of a lifetime and he really didn't want to miss out.

'See you in Russia!' said his Brazilian PSG teammates Neymar Jr, Thiago Silva and Marquinhos.

'See you in Russia!' said his Argentinian teammates Ángel and Giovani.

'See you in Russia!' said his Uruguayan teammate Edinson.

Kylian kept his fingers firmly crossed. He couldn't be the odd one out. France would need a young flair player in their squad! But had he done enough to show Deschamps that he was ready for Russia?

Maybe not in the World Cup qualifiers, but Kylian was still finding his feet at international level. There had been lots of exciting signs for the future. He hit the crossbar in a friendly against Wales, and then set up goals for Alexandre against Germany and Thomas against Colombia.

'Now you just need to start scoring goals for France like you do for PSG,' his younger brother Ethan said. He was now part of the club's youth team. 'I know you can do it!'

It was in the next friendly against the World Cup hosts Russia that Kylian had finally showed exactly what he was capable of. With Antoine and Olivier both on the bench, he was France's star striker and he was even wearing the Number 10 shirt. This was his big chance to impress his national team manager.

'Come on, let's show the old guys how it's done!' Kylian told his teammates Paul and Ousmane.

It was Paul who played the perfect pass to him just before half-time. Kylian sprinted between two defenders, cut inside and fired into the bottom corner. 1–0 to France!

Goooooooooooooooooooooaaaaaaaaaaaaaaaalllllllllllll llllllllllllllllll!!!!!!!!!!!!!!!!!!!

'Easy!' he said with a big smile as he high-fived Paul.

In the second half, Kylian scored again and it was one of his favourite goals ever. On the left side of the penalty area, he skilled the Russian defender in two stylish steps:

1) stepover,

2) nutmeg!

It was actually a double nutmeg because his shot then flew through the keeper's legs.

Goooooooooooooooooooooaaaaaaaaaaaaaaaalllllllllllll llllllllllllllllll!!!!!!!!!!!!!!!!!!!

The France fans in St Petersburg went wild for

Kylian's classic celebration.

'That's more like it, mate!' Paul teased, slapping his head playfully.

Deschamps was delighted with Kylian's performance. When he was substituted a few minutes later, he got a hug and a big pat on the back from his manager.

'When you play like that, you're unstoppable!'

That's why Kylian was feeling quietly confident as he waited for the France World Cup squad to be announced. With his speed and skill, his manager knew that he could be a real gamechanger.

At last, the list was out. The attackers would be: Antoine, Olivier, Ousmane, Nabil, Florian... and Kylian!

'My first World Cup,' he posted straight away on social media. 'A DREAM!'

When he first joined the national team, Kylian had felt like the new kid at school. Now, however, he couldn't wait to spend the summer with lots of his best friends in football. Benjamin, Thomas, Ousmane, Paul, Antoine – what a fun group of players France had!

Their World Cup preparations began at Kylian's old youth academy, Clairefontaine. They worked on their tactics and fitness, but most of all they worked on building up the team spirit.

'France feeling,' Benjamin wrote under an Instagram picture of him carrying Kylian around the training pitch on his back. In another photo, Kylian and Paul were wrestling each other on the grass.

Although they all had plenty of laughs together, the France players were deadly serious about winning the 2018 World Cup. Kylian hadn't played in the Euro 2016 final against Portugal but he still felt the pain of that disastrous defeat. It was their job to make the nation proud of their football team again.

Now that he was definitely in the squad, Kylian moved on to his next target – the first XI. After all, there was nothing he hated more than sitting on the boring bench!

Luckily for him, Kylian started all three of France's warm-up matches, and he scored in the last one against the USA. *Phew,* what a relief! So, would that be Deschamps' first-choice team, with Paul, N'Golo

Kanté and Blaise Matuidi in midfield, and Kylian, Antoine and Olivier in attack? He really hoped so.

When the squad numbers were announced, Kylian punched the air. He had got what he wanted – the Number 10 shirt! Everyone was happy: Paul had Number 6, Antoine had 7, Olivier had 9, Ousmane had 11 and Benjamin had 22.

'I've got a great feeling about this!' Kylian told his teammates as they set off for their World Cup adventure in Russia.

At their base camp in Moscow, the players had everything they needed – big luxurious beds, the best training facilities, and PlayStations for their competitive FIFA tournaments.

'Get comfortable because we're not going home until after we win the final!' Deschamps told his team confidently.

'Yeah!' they all cheered together.

France's first opponents in Group C would be Australia. They didn't have any famous superstars, but that didn't mean it would be an easy match; even Kylian knew that there was no such thing as an easy

World Cup match.

He waited impatiently for news of France's starting XI. At last, it arrived and it was… GOOD NEWS! He would be playing up front with Antoine and Ousmane.

'Come on!' Kylian shouted with his fists clenched.

What an honour it was to walk out onto the pitch and represent France at a World Cup. Kylian was desperate to make a big impact, but the Australia keeper saved his only shot of the first half.

'Keep making those runs!' Deschamps encouraged him.

Kylian did, but the pass never arrived. After seventy minutes, Olivier replaced Ousmane and rescued France. He used his strength to set up Paul's winning goal. What a relief! It had been a poor French performance but at least they had the victory they needed.

'We'll have to play way better than that against Peru,' captain Hugo Lloris warned them.

Deschamps' only change for that next game was moving Olivier into the starting line-up in place of

Ousmane. Phew! Kylian would have another chance
to prove that he was ready for Russia.

In the middle of the first half against Peru, Paul
won the ball in midfield and passed it through to
Olivier. His shot bounced off a Peru defender, over
the goalkeeper's head and straight to… Kylian! He
tapped the ball into the empty net. 1–0!

*Goooooooooooooooooooooaaaaaaaaaaaaaaaaaallllllllllll
lllllllllllllll!!!!!!!!!!!!!!!!!!!!!*

What an amazing moment! At the age of
nineteen, Kylian had his first ever World Cup goal!
Not only that, but he was now France's youngest
ever World Cup scorer. Hopefully he would score
better goals but there was plenty of time ahead for
that. For now, it was time to celebrate. Antoine
joined him and copied his classic pose – arms folded,
cool looks on their faces.

'*Allez Les Bleus! Allez Les Bleus!*' the fans chanted.

With Kylian off the mark, could France now go on
and win the whole World Cup?

CHAPTER 22

AMAZING VS ARGENTINA

Deschamps decided to rest Kylian for the final group match against Denmark. It was a wise move because he wanted his young superstar to be as fresh as possible for France's Round of 16 tie with Argentina.

For the Argentina game, Kylian couldn't wait to face his PSG teammates Ángel and Giovani and, of course, Argentina's Number 10, Lionel Messi. Yes, Cristiano had been Kylian's number one childhood hero but Messi was definitely in his top five. The guy was a total legend!

Times were changing, though. Messi was now thirty-one and Cristiano was thirty-three. Kylian, on the other hand, was only nineteen. People saw him as the future of world football but he wanted to be the present too. He was ready to become a World Cup star, and what better way to show it than by beating Messi's Argentina?

'Come on, if Croatia can thrash them, then so can we!' Paul argued.

Deschamps, however, wasn't getting carried away. 'Any team featuring Messi and Di Maria is dangerous,' the France manager warned his players. 'Of course we can beat them but we need to stay smart.'

The noise was deafening at the Kazan Arena as the two teams walked out for kick-off. France had far fewer fans than Argentina but they sang the national anthem as loudly as they could. Out on the pitch, Kylian did the same, just like he used to as a kid back in Bondy. He was so proud to represent his country at the World Cup.

Kylian started the game brilliantly. As soon as he got the ball, he turned and ZOOM! – he burst through the middle, dribbling all the way to the edge of the penalty area. Eventually, Javier Mascherano had to slide in and bring him down. Uh oh,

Argentina were in big trouble.

'Great work, mate!' Antoine clapped. His free kick bounced back off the crossbar. So close!

Never mind, France would get lots more chances because Kylian had done his homework. He knew that pace was Argentina's biggest weakness. At top speed, no-one would be able to catch him.

Five minutes later, Kylian got the ball deep in his own half, and ZOOM! he was off again...

past Éver Banega...

past Nicolás Tagliafico...

past Mascherano too.

What a run! Kylian only had the Argentina centre-back, Marcos Rojo, left to beat. No problem! He kicked the ball ahead of him and chased after it. In a sprint race, there was only going to be one winner. Rojo knew that and so he pulled Kylian to the floor. Penalty!

'Amazing! Are you alright?' Olivier asked as he helped his teammate up.

Kylian nodded glumly. It was so unfair; he was about to score another World Cup goal! At least

France had a penalty, and Antoine didn't miss. 1–0!

Kylian was having his best international match ever. A few minutes later, he sprinted through again and this time, he was fouled just outside the box. Unfortunately, Paul's free kick flew high and wide.

They could have been 3–0 up but instead, Ángel hit a stunning strike to make it 1–1 at half-time. Then, just after the restart, Argentina scored again. 2–1! Oh dear, suddenly France needed Kylian's magic more than ever.

Right-back Benjamin Pavard equalised for France with a glorious goal but they were playing knockout football now. If France didn't score another, the match would go to penalties…

No, Kylian wasn't going to let that happen. This was *his* World Cup. As the ball fell to him in the crowded box, he kept his cool.

First touch to control it,

Second touch to beat Rojo,

Third touch to shoot with his lethal left foot.

Gooooooooooooooooooooaaaaaaaaaaaaaaaalllllllllllll

lllllllllllllllll!!!!!!!!!!!!!!!!!!!!!

Kylian skidded across the grass on his knees, with his arms folded across his chest. No big deal! But it was a big deal; it was a *massive* deal. Soon Kylian was at the bottom of a full France squad hug, including all the substitutes.

'Nice one, *Casse-bonbon!*' Benjamin cheered.

Near the halfway line, Messi stared down at his feet, looking devastated.

'Watch out world – there's a new Number 10!' the commentator screamed on TV.

As Kylian jogged back for the restart, he bumped chests with Antoine. His confidence was sky-high and he wanted more. Just in case anyone had missed his first goal, he scored again four minutes later. Olivier fed the ball through and Kylian calmly buried it in the bottom corner. 4–2!

Goooooooooooooooooooaaaaaaaaaaaaaaaaaalllllllllll lllllllllllllll!!!!!!!!!!!!!!!!!!!!!

The substitutes raced back on to celebrate with France's new World Cup hero. Thanks to Kylian's amazing man-of-the-match performance, they were through to the quarter-finals! Kylian bumped chests with Ousmane, and then thanked Olivier with a hug and a high-five.

'This game will go down in history!' Antoine predicted.

It certainly would because Kylian had become only the second teenager ever to score two goals in a World Cup match. The first? None other than 'The King of Football' himself, Pelé, back in 1958. Wow, what an honour!

With five minutes to go, Deschamps gave Kylian a well-deserved rest. It wasn't a popular decision, however. The supporters wanted Kylian to continue and so did he. He was on a hat-trick, after all! As he trudged off slowly, his name echoed around the stadium.

Mbappé! Mbappé! Mbappé!

Kylian clapped the fans and then accepted a hug from his proud manager.

'Incredible!' was all Deschamps could say.

After the final whistle, Kylian walked around the pitch with a big smile on his face. He didn't want this amazing moment to ever end. He shook hands with all the Argentina players, including their Number 10.

'Well played,' Kylian said, seeing the despair on Messi's face. Football could be a very cruel game sometimes.

'You too,' the Argentinian replied graciously. 'You were the best player on the pitch today.'

Messi's brilliant football career was far from over but that night, a new world superstar was born.

CHAPTER 23

WORLD CHAMPION

'How are you feeling, Thirty-Seven?' Florian asked as the France players prepared for their World Cup quarter-final against Uruguay.

That was Kylian's new nickname because during that amazing match against Argentina, he had reached a top speed of 37 kilometres per hour. That was as fast as Usain Bolt in the Olympic 100-metre sprint!

'Put it this way; you'll be calling me Forty soon!' Kylian replied confidently.

His teammates were relying on him to be their speedy superstar again in the quarter-finals. It was going to be France's toughest test yet. Uruguay had two deadly duos: Diego Godín and José Giménez at the back, and Luis Suárez and Kylian's PSG teammate Edinson up front.

Uruguay had already knocked out Cristiano's Portugal and now they wanted to do the same to France. Even without the injured Edinson, they were still going to be very dangerous opponents.

'But if we stick to our gameplan, we'll win this,' Deschamps assured his players before kick-off.

That gameplan was simple – stay organised, work hard and work together.

Just like against Argentina, the France fans were outnumbered in the stadium. It sounded like the whole of South America had travelled to Russia for the summer! But Kylian wasn't going to let a loud crowd faze him. He was 100 per cent focused on his target – leading France into the World Cup semi-finals.

Every time Paul or Antoine got the ball in the middle, they tried to set him free on goal. Although Uruguay's defenders were excellent, no-one could keep up with a sprinting Kylian! Olivier tried to set him up too. After fifteen minutes, he headed the ball across goal to Kylian.

'Go on, score!' the France fans urged him. The Argentina match had showed that Kylian was capable of anything.

He had enough time to bring the ball down and shoot, but he didn't realise until it was too late. His header looped up and over the bar.

'Noooo!' Kylian groaned with his head in his hands. What a good chance wasted!

Oh well, there was still plenty of time to make up for his mistake. Kylian ran and ran but this time, he wasn't France's matchwinner. That was okay, though, because winning a World Cup was a team effort. Raphaël Varane and Antoine Griezmann scored the goals to beat Uruguay. 2–0 – job done!

'See you in the semi-finals,' Kylian wrote on Instagram with a big thumbs-up.

But who would their opponents be? On the journey back to base camp, many of the players relaxed by playing cards or watching a movie, but Kylian watched the other big quarter-final between Belgium and Neymar Jr's Brazil on his phone. It was important homework because France would have

to beat the winners. The match finished 2–1 to
Belgium.

'Bring it on!' Kylian told Antoine on the airplane
as he shared the news.

To become the best, France knew that they
would have to beat the best. Belgium had an
amazing attack too: Romelu Lukaku, Kevin de
Bruyne and Kylian's rival Number 10, Eden Hazard.
Wow, it was going to be a really great game.

Was Kylian feeling nervous ahead of the biggest
game of his life? No, instead he fell fast asleep on the
flight to St Petersburg! Benjamin took a sneaky photo
and posted it on social media.

'*Casse-bonbon* needs his beauty sleep for the big
match!' he joked.

In the World Cup semi-final, France stuck to
their gameplan once again. As soon as Paul got the
ball in midfield, ZOOM! Kylian was off, sprinting
between the Belgium centre-backs. He won that
race but sadly he couldn't quite beat their keeper
Thibaut Courtois to the pass.

'Nearly!' Kylian thought to himself as he jogged

back into position. He knew that in such a tight semi-final, one goal might be enough to win it.

France had to score first. Antoine played the ball over the top to Kylian who crossed it first-time to Olivier. He stretched out his left leg but his shot trickled wide. They both stood there with their hands on their heads. How many more glorious chances would they get?

Kylian slipped a pass through to Benjamin Pavard but Courtois made a great save.

'Not again!' Kylian muttered to himself. But just when his frustration was growing, France scored, when Antoine curled in a corner-kick and Samuel Umtiti headed it past Courtois. 1– 0!

Kylian grabbed the ball out of the net and booted it high into the air. 'Come on!' he screamed. France were forty minutes away from a place in the World Cup final.

Could they score a second goal to make things safe? Kylian flicked an incredible back-heel pass through to Olivier but his shot was blocked. In the end, it didn't matter because France held on until the final whistle.

Allez Les Bleus! Allez Les Bleus! Allez Les Bleus!

'Yesssss!' Kylian screamed, punching the air. All of the substitutes ran onto the pitch to join in the joyful celebrations. They were now only one step away from lifting the World Cup trophy.

'WHAT A DREAM!' Kylian wrote on Instagram next to photos from the match.

The stage was set for the biggest game of his career – France vs Croatia. At the age of nineteen, Kylian was about to play in his first World Cup final!

On the day of the final, he woke up with a phone full of good luck messages from friends, family, teammates and coaches. He didn't have time to reply to them all but they helped to fire Kylian up for his big day.

'Come on!' the France captain Hugo shouted, clapping his gloves together in the tunnel.

The atmosphere inside Moscow's Luzhniki Stadium was incredible. Supposedly, there were more Croatia fans than France fans, but you couldn't tell from the noise. Both national anthems were sung loudly and proudly. As the Croatia anthem ended, a roar went up around the stadium. It was time for the World Cup final to kick off!

The first half was full of drama but not for Kylian. The Croatia defence was keeping him quiet. Instead, it was Antoine who stole the show with a teasing free kick, and then a well-taken penalty. France 2 Croatia 1.

'We need to calm things down and take control of the game,' Deschamps told his players in the dressing room. 'Stay smart out there!'

That's exactly what France did in the second half. They were more solid in defence and they used Kylian's pace on the counter-attack.

Paul looked up and gave Kylian a great through-ball to chase onto. ZOOM! Kylian got there first, of course, and pulled it back to Antoine. He laid it off for Paul to strike. His first shot was poor but his second was perfect. 3–1!

Game over? No, there was still plenty of time left and Kylian was desperate to grab a goal of his own. When the ball came to him outside the box, he didn't hesitate. BANG! It was in the bottom corner before the keeper could even react.

Goooooooooooooooooooaaaaaaaaaaaaaaaaalllllllllll lllllllllllllll!!!!!!!!!!!!!!!!!!!!

There was just enough time for Kylian's trademark celebration pose before all his teammates jumped on him.

'You legend!'

'What a hit!'

'You did it, 37!'

Allez Les Bleus! Allez Les Bleus! Allez Les Bleus!

What a way for Kylian to end his terrific tournament! Four goals, twenty-one dribbles, one 37 kilometres-per-hour sprint, one Best Young Player award (although Croatia's Luka Modrić would win the Best Player award), and one World Cup winner's medal. All that and Kylian was now only the second teenager ever to score in a World Cup final. He was too old to beat Pelé's record, but the veteran 'King of Football' himself was still very impressed.

'Welcome to the club,' he messaged Kylian on social media, and then sent him a signed Santos shirt.

The next few days were a brilliant blur. But in between all the celebrations, Kylian found time to post not one but TWO photos of him kissing the World Cup trophy.

'HISTORY FOREVER!' he declared.

It took time for the achievement to really sink in – at nineteen years old, Kylian was already a World Champion.

'You might as well retire now!' his dad, Wilfried, joked.

Was there anything left for Kylian to win? Yes, plenty! Luckily, he was totally obsessed with that winning feeling.

After a short holiday in Ibiza, Kylian returned to Paris and moved straight on to his next target – winning the Champions League. Yes, the boy from Bondy had become a superstar, but he was only just getting started.

Turn the page for a sneak preview of another brilliant football story by Matt and Tom Oldfield. . .

NEYMAR

CHAPTER 1

OLYMPIC GOLD

'We have to win!' Neymar Jr told his teammates. He normally liked to laugh and dance before a match but not this time. He was captain and this was serious. 'Let's get revenge for the 2014 World Cup!'

Neymar Jr was the only member of Brazil's 2016 Olympic squad who had also been there for that awful night in Belo Horizonte two years earlier. When Germany thrashed Brazil 7–1 in the semi-finals on home soil, the whole nation was left heartbroken. Football was their greatest passion.

But it hurt Neymar Jr more than most because he was injured for that game and couldn't be the national hero that they needed. This time, though, as they faced Germany once again, he was fit and raring to go.

'Germany better watch out!' his strike partner, Gabriel Jesus cheered.

After a long season at Barcelona, Neymar Jr had taken a little while to find his form at the Olympics. As the one of the oldest players in the squad, his teammates depended on him. It was a lot of responsibility and after three matches, Neymar Jr hadn't scored a single goal.

'Don't worry,' the coach Rogério Micale told him. 'That was your warm-up; now we need you at your best in these next big games!'

Neymar Jr scored one against Colombia in the quarter-finals, then two against Honduras in the semi-finals. He had rediscovered his *ginga* rhythm, his Brazilian flair, just in time.

'That means you should score a hat-trick in the final!' his teammate Marquinhos joked.

'No pressure, then!' Neymar Jr replied with a smile on his face.

He led the players out on to the pitch to face

Germany at the Maracanã Stadium in Rio de Janeiro. Nearly 60,000 Brazilians had come to cheer on their country, wearing the famous yellow shirt and waving yellow-and-green flags. They were ready for a party, and the noise and colour were incredible.

Neymar Jr stood with his hand on his heart and sang the national anthem loudly. He was so proud to represent his nation and he was one win away from making everyone very happy. He couldn't wait.

Midway through the first half, Brazil won a free kick just outside the penalty area. It was a perfect opportunity for Neymar Jr. He placed the ball down, stepped back and took a long, deep breath. Then he curled the ball powerfully towards the top corner. It was too quick and high for the goalkeeper to save. The shot hit the underside of the crossbar and bounced down into the back of the net.

Gooooooooooooooooaaaaaaaaaaaaaaaaaaalllllllllllllllll lllllllllllll!!!!!!!!!!!!!!!!!!!!

Neymar Jr had always dreamed of scoring amazing goals in international finals. Now it was a reality and he would never forget the moment. All of his teammates ran over and jumped on him.

'You did it!' Gabriel shouted.

After the celebrations, Neymar Jr told the others to calm down and focus. 'We haven't won this yet – concentrate!'

Brazil defended well but after sixty minutes, Germany equalised. Neymar Jr had more work to do. He dribbled past one defender and then dropped in a clever Cruyff Turn to wrong-foot a second. It was magical skill and the crowd loved it. He now had the space to shoot. The ball swerved past the goalkeeper's outstretched arm but just wide of the post.

'So close!' Neymar Jr said to himself, putting his hands on his head.

Brazil attacked again and again but they couldn't find a winning goal, even after thirty minutes of extra-time. It was time for penalties.

'I'll take the last one,' Neymar Jr told Micale. He was determined to be the national hero this time.

After eight penalties, it was 4–4. When Brazil's goalkeeper Weverton saved the ninth spot-kick, Neymar Jr had his golden chance. He walked from the halfway line towards the penalty spot with thousands of fans cheering his name.

He picked up the ball, kissed it and put it back down. As he waited for the referee's whistle, he tried to slow his heartbeat down. If he was too excited, he might kick it over the bar. He needed to be his normal, cool self.

As he ran up, he slowed down to try to make the German goalkeeper move early. The keeper dived low to the right and Neymar Jr put his shot high and to the left. As the ball went in, Neymar burst into tears of joy. He had led his country all the way to the Olympic Gold Medal for the first time ever. As he fell to his knees and thanked God, the other Brazil players ran to hug their hero.

'You always said that we could do it!' his teammate Luan shouted. 'Now it's carnival time!'

As Neymar Jr got back on his feet, he listened to the incredible noise of the Maracanã crowd. It was the best thing he had ever heard.

'Imagine what the atmosphere would have been like if we'd made it to the World Cup final and won it in 2014!' Neymar Jr thought to himself, but it was time to forget about the pains of the past and move forward. Thanks to him, his country was back at the top of world football again.

'Thank you!' the coach Micale said to him, giving him the biggest hug of all.

He was still only twenty-four but Neymar Jr had already been Brazil's number one superstar for years. There was so much pressure on him but he refused to let his country down, even after moving to Spain to play for Barcelona.

Neymar Jr had Brazil to thank for everything: the love of his family and friends; the support of his coaches at Portuguesa Santista and Santos; and above all, the amazing skills that he had first developed in street football, beach football and *futsal* matches in São Paulo.

KYLIAN MBAPPÉ
HONOURS

Monaco

🏆 Ligue 1: 2016–17

🏆 French Youth Cup: 2015–16

Paris Saint-Germain

🏆 Ligue 1: 2017–18, 2018–19, 2019–20,
2021–22

🏆 French Cup: 2017–18, 2019–20, 2020–21

🏆 League Cup: 2017–18, 2019–20,

🏆 French Super Cup: 2018–19, 2019–20,
2020–21

France U19

🏆 UEFA European Under-19 Championship: 2016

France

🏆 FIFA World Cup: 2018

🏆 UEFA Nations League: 2021

Individual

🏆 UEFA European Under-19 Championship Team of the Tournament: 2016

🏆 UNFP Ligue 1 Young Player of the Year: 2016–17, 2017–18

🏆 UNFP Ligue 1 Team of the Year: 2016–17, 2017–18

🏆 UEFA Champions League Team of the Season: 2016–17

🏆 FIFA FIFPro World XI: 2018, 2019

🏆 Golden Boy: 2017

🏆 FIFA World Cup Best Young Player Award: 2018

MBAPPE

7 & 10

THE FACTS

NAME: Kylian Mbappé

DATE OF BIRTH: 20 December 1998

PLACE OF BIRTH: Bondy

NATIONALITY: French

BEST FRIEND: Achraf Hakimi

CURRENT CLUB: PSG

POSITION: CF

THE STATS

Height (cm):	178
Club appearances:	296
Club goals:	215
Club assists:	107
Club trophies:	15
International appearances:	59
International goals:	28
International trophies:	3
Ballon d'Ors:	0

★ ★ ★ **HERO RATING: 89** ★ ★ ★

GREATEST MOMENTS

20 FEBRUARY 2016, MONACO 3–1 TROYES

Just months after his first-team debut and his seventeenth birthday, Kylian achieved his next target – his first senior goal! It wasn't his best strike but it still meant the world to him because he had just become Monaco's youngest-ever goalscorer! And whose record had Kylian broken? Yes, that's right, his French hero, Thierry Henry. A new superstar was born.

21 FEBRUARY 2017,
MANCHESTER CITY 5–3 MONACO

This was the night when Kylian went from being the talk of French football to the talk of world football. It was Manchester City who won this game, but Kylian's speed and skill caused them all kinds of problems. He even had the composure to score a fantastic first European goal.

31 MARCH 2018,
PSG 3–0 MONACO

Kylian made the big-money move to PSG in order to win more top trophies. In their first season together, 'MCN' didn't win the Champions League but they did win the French treble. Kylian was the man of the match in this League Cup final against his old club, Monaco. He won an early penalty with one of his deadly dribbles, and then set up goals for Ángel and Edinson. Neymar who?!

30 JUNE 2018, FRANCE 4–3 ARGENTINA

Kylian's match-winning performance against Lionel Messi's Argentina will go down in World Cup history. His phenomenal pace won France an early penalty and in the second half, his two excellent finishes sent them through to the quarter-finals. Kylian became the first teenager since 'The King of Football', Pelé, to score a World Cup double.

15 JULY 2018, FRANCE 4–2 CROATIA

Kylian wasn't at his awesome best against Croatia but he still got what he wanted – a World Cup final goal and a World Cup winner's medal. In the second half, Kylian got the ball just outside the box and buried his shot in the bottom corner. GOAL – what a way to finish off his first fantastic tournament for France!

PLAY LIKE YOUR HEROES

THE KYLIAN MBAPPÉ
SPRINT DRIBBLE

STEP 1: Track back to help your team in defence. It gives you more space for your sprint dribble!

STEP 2: Stay alert at all times. If an opponent plays a bad pass or your team wins the ball, you've got to be ready for the race...

STEP 3: ZOOM! Your first burst of speed is really important. Power your way past as many defenders as possible.

STEP 4: Okay, who's left? If you can beat the last defenders with pure pace, go for it!

STEP 5: If not, you'll need to use your silky skills. Stepover, stepover, stepover, ZOOM!

STEP 6: You're one-on-one with the keeper now, so you've got to stay calm. Pick your spot and shoot.

STEP 7: GOAL! It's celebration time. Run over to the fans, fold your arms across your chest and remember to look as cool as you can.

TEST YOUR KNOWLEDGE

1. What sport did Kylian's mum play?

2. Who was Kylian's number-one childhood hero?

3. Which two top European clubs did Kylian visit before joining Monaco?

4. How old was Kylian when he made his Monaco first-team debut?

5. What was the name of Kylian's strike partner as France won the Under-19 Euros?

6. What was the name of Kylian's strike partner as Monaco won the Ligue 1 title?

7. Which country did Kylian make his senior France debut against?

8. Name two clubs (other than PSG!) who tried to sign Kylian in Summer 2018?

9. Kylian won four trophies in his first season at PSG – true or false?

10. How many goals did Kylian score at the 2018 World Cup?

11. Kylian won the FIFA World Cup Best Young Player award, but who won the FIFA Men's Player of the Year award?

Answers below. . . No cheating!

1. Handball 2. Cristiano Ronaldo 3. Chelsea and Real Madrid 4. 16 (16 years and 347 days to be exact!) 5. Jean-Kévin Augustin 6. Radamel Falcao 7. Luxembourg 8. Any of Arsenal, Liverpool, Manchester City and Real Madrid 9. False – he only won three but he posed with all four of PSG's trophies anyway! 10. Four 11. Luka Modrić